_____

_____

_____

"Traveling leaves you speechless,

then turns you into a storyteller."

- Ibn Battuta

Date: _____ From: _____ Beginning Mileage: _____

Weather: To: _____ Ending Mileage: _____

☀ ☁ ☔ ❄ Route Taken: _____

🌡 🌡 📢 ☁ _____ Total Miles Traveled: _____

Campground Information

Name: _____ Our Rating: ☆ ☆ ☆ ☆ ☆

Address: _____ GPS: _____

Phone: _____ Altitude: _____

Site # _____ $ _____ ☐ Day ☐ Week ☐ Month   Cell Service / Carrier: _____

☐ First Visit ☐ Return Visit ☐ Easy Access   ☐ Antenna Reception ☐ Satellite TV ☐ Cable TV
☐ Site Level ☐ Back-in ☐ Pull-through   ☐ Wifi Available ☐ Free ☐ Fee $ _____
☐ 15 amp ☐ 30 amp ☐ 50 amp
☐ Water ☐ Sewer ☐ Shade ☐ Sun   Memberships: _____
☐ Paved ☐ Sand / Grass ☐ Gravel   Ammenities: _____
☐ Picnic Table ☐ Fire ring ☐ Trees ☐ Lawn
☐ Patio ☐ Kid Friendly ☐ Pet Friendly   Location ☺ ☺ ☹   Water Pressure ☺ ☺ ☹
☐ Store ☐ Cafe ☐ Firewood   Restrooms ☺ ☺ ☹   Laundry ☺ ☺ ☹
☐ Ice ☐ Security ☐ Quiet ☐ Noisy   Pool ☺ ☺ ☹   Hot Tub ☺ ☺ ☹

Places Visited / Activities: _____

_____

_____

_____

People Met / New Friends: _____

_____

_____

_____

Food, Dining & Restaurants: _____

_____

_____

_____

Highlights / Memorable Events: _____

_____

_____

_____

Places To Go & Things To Do for Next Time: _____

_____

_____

_____

NOTES:

Date:	From:	Beginning Mileage:
Weather:	To:	Ending Mileage:
☀ ⛅ ☂ ❄	Route Taken:	Total Miles Traveled:
🌡 🌡 🚩 ☁		

CAMPGROUND INFORMATION

Name:_____

Address:_____

Phone:_____

Site #_____ $_____ ☐ Day ☐ Week ☐ Month

☐ First Visit   ☐ Return Visit   ☐ Easy Access
☐ Site Level   ☐ Back-in   ☐ Pull-through
☐ 15 amp   ☐ 30 amp   ☐ 50 amp
☐ Water   ☐ Sewer   ☐ Shade   ☐ Sun
☐ Paved   ☐ Sand / Grass   ☐ Gravel
☐ Picnic Table   ☐ Fire ring   ☐ Trees   ☐ Lawn
☐ Patio   ☐ Kid Friendly   ☐ Pet Friendly
☐ Store   ☐ Cafe   ☐ Firewood
☐ Ice   ☐ Security   ☐ Quiet   ☐ Noisy

Our Rating: ☆ ☆ ☆ ☆ ☆

GPS: _____

Altitude: _____

Cell Service / Carrier:_____

☐ Antenna Reception   ☐ Satellite TV   ☐ Cable TV
☐ Wifi Available   ☐ Free ☐ Fee $_____

Memberships: _____

Ammenities:_____

Location	☺ ☺ ☹	Water Pressure	☺ ☺ ☹
Restrooms	☺ ☺ ☹	Laundry	☺ ☺ ☹
Pool	☺ ☺ ☹	Hot Tub	☺ ☺ ☹

PLACES VISITED / ACTIVITIES: _____

_____
_____
_____

PEOPLE MET / NEW FRIENDS: _____

_____
_____
_____

FOOD, DINING & RESTAURANTS: _____

_____
_____
_____

HIGHLIGHTS / MEMORABLE EVENTS: _____

_____
_____
_____

PLACES TO GO & THINGS TO DO FOR NEXT TIME: _____

_____
_____
_____

NOTES:

Date: _____

Weather:

☀ ☁ ☂ ❄

🌡 ❄🌡 🚩 ☁

From: _____

To: _____

Route Taken: _____

_____

Beginning Mileage:

_____

Ending Mileage:

_____

Total Miles Traveled:

_____

CAMPGROUND INFORMATION

Name: _____

Address: _____

Phone: _____

Site # _____ $ _____ ☐ Day ☐ Week ☐ Month

☐ First Visit ☐ Return Visit ☐ Easy Access
☐ Site Level ☐ Back-in ☐ Pull-through
☐ 15 amp ☐ 30 amp ☐ 50 amp
☐ Water ☐ Sewer ☐ Shade ☐ Sun
☐ Paved ☐ Sand / Grass ☐ Gravel
☐ Picnic Table ☐ Fire ring ☐ Trees ☐ Lawn
☐ Patio ☐ Kid Friendly ☐ Pet Friendly
☐ Store ☐ Cafe ☐ Firewood
☐ Ice ☐ Security ☐ Quiet ☐ Noisy

Our Rating: ☆ ☆ ☆ ☆ ☆

GPS: _____

Altitude: _____

Cell Service / Carrier: _____

☐ Antenna Reception ☐ Satellite TV ☐ Cable TV
☐ Wifi Available ☐ Free ☐ Fee $ _____

Memberships: _____

Ammenities: _____

Location	☺	☺	☹	Water Pressure	☺	☺	☹
Restrooms	☺	☺	☹	Laundry	☺	☺	☹
Pool	☺	☺	☹	Hot Tub	☺	☺	☹

PLACES VISITED / ACTIVITIES: _____

_____

_____

_____

PEOPLE MET / NEW FRIENDS: _____

_____

_____

_____

FOOD, DINING & RESTAURANTS: _____

_____

_____

_____

HIGHLIGHTS / MEMORABLE EVENTS: _____

_____

_____

_____

PLACES TO GO & THINGS TO DO FOR NEXT TIME: _____

_____

_____

_____

NOTES:

Date: _____	From: _____	Beginning Mileage:
Weather:	To: _____	_____
☀ ⛅ ⛈ ❄	Route Taken: _____	Ending Mileage:
🌡 🌡 🏴 🌀	_____	_____ Total Miles Traveled:

CAMPGROUND INFORMATION

Name:_____	Our Rating: ☆ ☆ ☆ ☆ ☆
Address:_____	GPS: _____
Phone:_____	Altitude: _____
Site #_____ $_____ ☐ Day ☐ Week ☐ Month	Cell Service / Carrier:_____

☐ First Visit	☐ Return Visit	☐ Easy Access
☐ Site Level	☐ Back-in	☐ Pull-through
☐ 15 amp	☐ 30 amp	☐ 50 amp
☐ Water	☐ Sewer	☐ Shade ☐ Sun
☐ Paved	☐ Sand / Grass	☐ Gravel
☐ Picnic Table	☐ Fire ring	☐ Trees ☐ Lawn
☐ Patio	☐ Kid Friendly	☐ Pet Friendly
☐ Store	☐ Cafe	☐ Firewood
☐ Ice	☐ Security	☐ Quiet ☐ Noisy

☐ Antenna Reception ☐ Satellite TV ☐ Cable TV
☐ Wifi Available ☐ Free ☐ Fee $_____

Memberships: _____

Ammenities:_____

Location	☺	😐	☹	Water Pressure	☺	😐	☹
Restrooms	☺	😐	☹	Laundry	☺	😐	☹
Pool	☺	😐	☹	Hot Tub	☺	😐	☹

PLACES VISITED / ACTIVITIES: _____
_____
_____
_____

PEOPLE MET / NEW FRIENDS: _____
_____
_____
_____

FOOD, DINING & RESTAURANTS: _____
_____
_____
_____

HIGHLIGHTS / MEMORABLE EVENTS: _____
_____
_____
_____

PLACES TO GO & THINGS TO DO FOR NEXT TIME: _____
_____
_____
_____

NOTES:

Date: _____

Weather:

☀ ☁ ☂ ❄

🌡 🌡 📢 ☁

From: _____

To: _____

Route Taken: _____

_____

Beginning Mileage: _____

Ending Mileage: _____

Total Miles Traveled: _____

CAMPGROUND INFORMATION

Name: _____

Address: _____

Phone: _____

Site # _____ $ _____ ☐ Day ☐ Week ☐ Month

☐ First Visit   ☐ Return Visit   ☐ Easy Access
☐ Site Level   ☐ Back-in   ☐ Pull-through
☐ 15 amp   ☐ 30 amp   ☐ 50 amp
☐ Water   ☐ Sewer   ☐ Shade   ☐ Sun
☐ Paved   ☐ Sand / Grass   ☐ Gravel
☐ Picnic Table   ☐ Fire ring   ☐ Trees   ☐ Lawn
☐ Patio   ☐ Kid Friendly   ☐ Pet Friendly
☐ Store   ☐ Cafe   ☐ Firewood
☐ Ice   ☐ Security   ☐ Quiet   ☐ Noisy

Our Rating: ☆ ☆ ☆ ☆ ☆

GPS: _____

Altitude: _____

Cell Service / Carrier: _____

☐ Antenna Reception   ☐ Satellite TV   ☐ Cable TV
☐ Wifi Available   ☐ Free ☐ Fee $ _____

Memberships: _____

Ammenities: _____

Location	☺	😐	☹	Water Pressure	☺	😐	☹
Restrooms	☺	😐	☹	Laundry	☺	😐	☹
Pool	☺	😐	☹	Hot Tub	☺	😐	☹

PLACES VISITED / ACTIVITIES: _____

_____

_____

_____

PEOPLE MET / NEW FRIENDS: _____

_____

_____

_____

FOOD, DINING & RESTAURANTS: _____

_____

_____

_____

HIGHLIGHTS / MEMORABLE EVENTS: _____

_____

_____

_____

PLACES TO GO & THINGS TO DO FOR NEXT TIME: _____

_____

_____

_____

NOTES:

Date: _____	From: _____	Beginning Mileage:
Weather:	To: _____	_____
☀ ⛅ ☔ ❄	Route Taken: _____	Ending Mileage:
🌡 🌡 📯 ☁	_____	_____
		Total Miles Traveled:

CAMPGROUND INFORMATION

Name:_____   Our Rating: ☆ ☆ ☆ ☆ ☆

Address:_____   GPS: _____

Phone:_____   Altitude: _____

Site #_____ $_____ ☐ Day ☐ Week ☐ Month   Cell Service / Carrier:_____

☐ First Visit   ☐ Return Visit   ☐ Easy Access   ☐ Antenna Reception ☐ Satellite TV ☐ Cable TV
☐ Site Level   ☐ Back-in   ☐ Pull-through   ☐ Wifi Available   ☐ Free ☐ Fee $_____
☐ 15 amp   ☐ 30 amp   ☐ 50 amp
☐ Water   ☐ Sewer   ☐ Shade ☐ Sun   Memberships: _____
☐ Paved   ☐ Sand / Grass   ☐ Gravel   Ammenities:_____
☐ Picnic Table ☐ Fire ring   ☐ Trees ☐ Lawn
☐ Patio   ☐ Kid Friendly   ☐ Pet Friendly   Location   ☺ ☺ ☹   Water Pressure ☺ ☺ ☹
☐ Store   ☐ Cafe   ☐ Firewood   Restrooms ☺ ☺ ☹   Laundry   ☺ ☺ ☹
☐ Ice   ☐ Security   ☐ Quiet ☐ Noisy Pool   ☺ ☺ ☹   Hot Tub   ☺ ☺ ☹

PLACES VISITED / ACTIVITIES: _____

_____

_____

_____

PEOPLE MET / NEW FRIENDS: _____

_____

_____

_____

FOOD, DINING & RESTAURANTS: _____

_____

_____

_____

HIGHLIGHTS / MEMORABLE EVENTS: _____

_____

_____

_____

PLACES TO GO & THINGS TO DO FOR NEXT TIME: _____

_____

_____

_____

NOTES:

Date: _____

Weather:

☀ ☁ ☂ ❄

🌡 ❄🌡 🚩 ☁

From: _____

To: _____

Route Taken: _____

_____

Beginning Mileage:
_____

Ending Mileage:
_____

Total Miles Traveled:
_____

CAMPGROUND INFORMATION

Name: _____

Address: _____

Phone: _____

Site # _____ $ _____ ☐ Day ☐ Week ☐ Month

☐ First Visit   ☐ Return Visit   ☐ Easy Access
☐ Site Level   ☐ Back-in   ☐ Pull-through
☐ 15 amp   ☐ 30 amp   ☐ 50 amp
☐ Water   ☐ Sewer   ☐ Shade ☐ Sun
☐ Paved   ☐ Sand / Grass   ☐ Gravel
☐ Picnic Table   ☐ Fire ring   ☐ Trees ☐ Lawn
☐ Patio   ☐ Kid Friendly   ☐ Pet Friendly
☐ Store   ☐ Cafe   ☐ Firewood
☐ Ice   ☐ Security   ☐ Quiet ☐ Noisy

Our Rating: ☆ ☆ ☆ ☆ ☆

GPS: _____

Altitude: _____

Cell Service / Carrier: _____

☐ Antenna Reception   ☐ Satellite TV   ☐ Cable TV
☐ Wifi Available   ☐ Free ☐ Fee $ _____

Memberships: _____

Ammenities: _____

	☺ ☺ ☹		☺ ☺ ☹
Location	☺ ☺ ☹	Water Pressure	☺ ☺ ☹
Restrooms	☺ ☺ ☹	Laundry	☺ ☺ ☹
Pool	☺ ☺ ☹	Hot Tub	☺ ☺ ☹

PLACES VISITED / ACTIVITIES: _____

_____

_____

_____

PEOPLE MET / NEW FRIENDS: _____

_____

_____

_____

FOOD, DINING & RESTAURANTS: _____

_____

_____

_____

HIGHLIGHTS / MEMORABLE EVENTS: _____

_____

_____

_____

PLACES TO GO & THINGS TO DO FOR NEXT TIME: _____

_____

_____

_____

NOTES:

Date: _____	From: _____	Beginning Mileage:
Weather:	To: _____	_____
☀ ⛅ ☔ ❄	Route Taken: _____	Ending Mileage:
🌡 🌡 📢 ☁	_____	_____
		Total Miles Traveled:

CAMPGROUND INFORMATION

Name:_____	Our Rating: ☆ ☆ ☆ ☆ ☆
Address:_____	GPS: _____
Phone:_____	Altitude: _____
Site #_____ $_____ ☐ Day ☐ Week ☐ Month	Cell Service / Carrier:_____

Site attributes:
- ☐ First Visit ☐ Return Visit ☐ Easy Access
- ☐ Site Level ☐ Back-in ☐ Pull-through
- ☐ 15 amp ☐ 30 amp ☐ 50 amp
- ☐ Water ☐ Sewer ☐ Shade ☐ Sun
- ☐ Paved ☐ Sand / Grass ☐ Gravel
- ☐ Picnic Table ☐ Fire ring ☐ Trees ☐ Lawn
- ☐ Patio ☐ Kid Friendly ☐ Pet Friendly
- ☐ Store ☐ Cafe ☐ Firewood
- ☐ Ice ☐ Security ☐ Quiet ☐ Noisy

Connectivity:
- ☐ Antenna Reception ☐ Satellite TV ☐ Cable TV
- ☐ Wifi Available ☐ Free ☐ Fee $_____

Memberships: _____

Ammenities:_____

Location	☺	☺	☹	Water Pressure	☺	☺	☹
Restrooms	☺	☺	☹	Laundry	☺	☺	☹
Pool	☺	☺	☹	Hot Tub	☺	☺	☹

PLACES VISITED / ACTIVITIES: _____
_____
_____
_____

PEOPLE MET / NEW FRIENDS: _____
_____
_____
_____

FOOD, DINING & RESTAURANTS: _____
_____
_____
_____

HIGHLIGHTS / MEMORABLE EVENTS: _____
_____
_____

PLACES TO GO & THINGS TO DO FOR NEXT TIME: _____
_____
_____
_____

NOTES:

Date: _____

Weather:
☀ ⛅ 🌧 ❄
🌡 🌡 📢 ☁

From: _____

To: _____

Route Taken: _____

_____

_____

Beginning Mileage:
_____

Ending Mileage:
_____

Total Miles Traveled:
_____

CAMPGROUND INFORMATION

Name: _____

Address: _____

Phone: _____

Site # _____ $ _____ ☐ Day ☐ Week ☐ Month

☐ First Visit   ☐ Return Visit   ☐ Easy Access
☐ Site Level   ☐ Back-in   ☐ Pull-through
☐ 15 amp   ☐ 30 amp   ☐ 50 amp
☐ Water   ☐ Sewer   ☐ Shade   ☐ Sun
☐ Paved   ☐ Sand / Grass   ☐ Gravel
☐ Picnic Table ☐ Fire ring   ☐ Trees   ☐ Lawn
☐ Patio   ☐ Kid Friendly   ☐ Pet Friendly
☐ Store   ☐ Cafe   ☐ Firewood
☐ Ice   ☐ Security   ☐ Quiet   ☐ Noisy

Our Rating: ☆ ☆ ☆ ☆ ☆

GPS: _____

Altitude: _____

Cell Service / Carrier: _____

☐ Antenna Reception   ☐ Satellite TV   ☐ Cable TV
☐ Wifi Available   ☐ Free ☐ Fee $ _____

Memberships: _____

Ammenities: _____

Location	☺	😐	☹	Water Pressure	☺	😐	☹
Restrooms	☺	😐	☹	Laundry	☺	😐	☹
Pool	☺	😐	☹	Hot Tub	☺	😐	☹

PLACES VISITED / ACTIVITIES: _____

_____

_____

_____

PEOPLE MET / NEW FRIENDS: _____

_____

_____

_____

FOOD, DINING & RESTAURANTS: _____

_____

_____

_____

HIGHLIGHTS / MEMORABLE EVENTS: _____

_____

_____

_____

PLACES TO GO & THINGS TO DO FOR NEXT TIME: _____

_____

_____

_____

NOTES:

Date: _____	From: _____	Beginning Mileage:
Weather:	To: _____	_____
☀ ☁ ☂ ❄	Route Taken: _____	Ending Mileage:
🌡 🌡 🚩 ☁	_____	_____
		Total Miles Traveled:
		_____

CAMPGROUND INFORMATION

Name: _____

Our Rating: ☆ ☆ ☆ ☆ ☆

Address: _____

GPS: _____

Phone: _____

Altitude: _____

Site # _____ $ _____ ☐ Day ☐ Week ☐ Month

Cell Service / Carrier: _____

☐ First Visit	☐ Return Visit	☐ Easy Access
☐ Site Level	☐ Back-in	☐ Pull-through
☐ 15 amp	☐ 30 amp	☐ 50 amp
☐ Water	☐ Sewer	☐ Shade ☐ Sun
☐ Paved	☐ Sand / Grass	☐ Gravel
☐ Picnic Table	☐ Fire ring	☐ Trees ☐ Lawn
☐ Patio	☐ Kid Friendly	☐ Pet Friendly
☐ Store	☐ Cafe	☐ Firewood
☐ Ice	☐ Security	☐ Quiet ☐ Noisy

☐ Antenna Reception   ☐ Satellite TV   ☐ Cable TV
☐ Wifi Available   ☐ Free   ☐ Fee $ _____

Memberships: _____

Ammenities: _____

Location	☺ ☺ ☹	Water Pressure	☺ ☺ ☹
Restrooms	☺ ☺ ☹	Laundry	☺ ☺ ☹
Pool	☺ ☺ ☹	Hot Tub	☺ ☺ ☹

PLACES VISITED / ACTIVITIES: _____

_____
_____
_____

PEOPLE MET / NEW FRIENDS: _____

_____
_____
_____

FOOD, DINING & RESTAURANTS: _____

_____
_____
_____

HIGHLIGHTS / MEMORABLE EVENTS: _____

_____
_____
_____

PLACES TO GO & THINGS TO DO FOR NEXT TIME: _____

_____
_____
_____

NOTES:

Date: _____

Weather:

☀ ⛅ ☂ ❄

🌡 🌡 📯 ☁

From: _____

To: _____

Route Taken: _____

_____

Beginning Mileage: _____

Ending Mileage: _____

Total Miles Traveled: _____

Campground Information

Name: _____

Address: _____

Phone: _____

Site # _____ $_____ ☐ Day ☐ Week ☐ Month

☐ First Visit   ☐ Return Visit   ☐ Easy Access
☐ Site Level   ☐ Back-in   ☐ Pull-through
☐ 15 amp   ☐ 30 amp   ☐ 50 amp
☐ Water   ☐ Sewer   ☐ Shade   ☐ Sun
☐ Paved   ☐ Sand / Grass   ☐ Gravel
☐ Picnic Table   ☐ Fire ring   ☐ Trees   ☐ Lawn
☐ Patio   ☐ Kid Friendly   ☐ Pet Friendly
☐ Store   ☐ Cafe   ☐ Firewood
☐ Ice   ☐ Security   ☐ Quiet   ☐ Noisy

Our Rating: ☆ ☆ ☆ ☆ ☆

GPS: _____

Altitude: _____

Cell Service / Carrier: _____

☐ Antenna Reception   ☐ Satellite TV   ☐ Cable TV
☐ Wifi Available   ☐ Free ☐ Fee $_____

Memberships: _____

Ammenities: _____

Location	☺	☹	Water Pressure	☺	☹
Restrooms	☺	☹	Laundry	☺	☹
Pool	☺	☹	Hot Tub	☺	☹

Places Visited / Activities: _____

_____

_____

_____

People Met / New Friends: _____

_____

_____

_____

Food, Dining & Restaurants: _____

_____

_____

_____

Highlights / Memorable Events: _____

_____

_____

_____

Places To Go & Things To Do for Next Time: _____

_____

_____

_____

NOTES:

Date: _____

Weather:

☀ ⛅ ☔ ❄
🌡 🌡 🚩 ☁

From: _____

To: _____

Route Taken: _____

_____

Beginning Mileage:
_____

Ending Mileage:
_____

Total Miles Traveled:

CAMPGROUND INFORMATION

Name: _____

Address: _____

Phone: _____

Site # _____ $ _____ ☐ Day ☐ Week ☐ Month

☐ First Visit ☐ Return Visit ☐ Easy Access
☐ Site Level ☐ Back-in ☐ Pull-through
☐ 15 amp ☐ 30 amp ☐ 50 amp
☐ Water ☐ Sewer ☐ Shade ☐ Sun
☐ Paved ☐ Sand / Grass ☐ Gravel
☐ Picnic Table ☐ Fire ring ☐ Trees ☐ Lawn
☐ Patio ☐ Kid Friendly ☐ Pet Friendly
☐ Store ☐ Cafe ☐ Firewood
☐ Ice ☐ Security ☐ Quiet ☐ Noisy

Our Rating: ☆ ☆ ☆ ☆ ☆

GPS: _____

Altitude: _____

Cell Service / Carrier: _____

☐ Antenna Reception ☐ Satellite TV ☐ Cable TV
☐ Wifi Available ☐ Free ☐ Fee $ _____

Memberships: _____

Ammenities: _____

Location	☺	😐	☹	Water Pressure	☺	😐	☹
Restrooms	☺	😐	☹	Laundry	☺	😐	☹
Pool	☺	😐	☹	Hot Tub	☺	😐	☹

PLACES VISITED / ACTIVITIES: _____

_____

_____

_____

PEOPLE MET / NEW FRIENDS: _____

_____

_____

_____

FOOD, DINING & RESTAURANTS: _____

_____

_____

_____

HIGHLIGHTS / MEMORABLE EVENTS: _____

_____

_____

_____

PLACES TO GO & THINGS TO DO FOR NEXT TIME: _____

_____

_____

_____

NOTES:

Date: _____	From: _____	Beginning Mileage:
	To: _____	_____
Weather:	Route Taken: _____	Ending Mileage:
☀ ☁ ☂ ❄	_____	_____
🌡 🌡 🚩 ☁		Total Miles Traveled:

CAMPGROUND INFORMATION

Name:_____	Our Rating: ☆ ☆ ☆ ☆ ☆
Address:_____	GPS: _____
Phone:_____	Altitude: _____
Site #_____ $_____ ☐ Day ☐ Week ☐ Month	Cell Service / Carrier:_____

☐ First Visit	☐ Return Visit	☐ Easy Access
☐ Site Level	☐ Back-in	☐ Pull-through
☐ 15 amp	☐ 30 amp	☐ 50 amp
☐ Water	☐ Sewer	☐ Shade ☐ Sun
☐ Paved	☐ Sand / Grass	☐ Gravel
☐ Picnic Table	☐ Fire ring	☐ Trees ☐ Lawn
☐ Patio	☐ Kid Friendly	☐ Pet Friendly
☐ Store	☐ Cafe	☐ Firewood
☐ Ice	☐ Security	☐ Quiet ☐ Noisy

☐ Antenna Reception ☐ Satellite TV ☐ Cable TV
☐ Wifi Available ☐ Free ☐ Fee $_____
Memberships: _____
Ammenities:_____

Location	☺ ☺ ☹	Water Pressure	☺ ☺ ☹
Restrooms	☺ ☺ ☹	Laundry	☺ ☺ ☹
Pool	☺ ☺ ☹	Hot Tub	☺ ☺ ☹

PLACES VISITED / ACTIVITIES: _____

_____

_____

_____

PEOPLE MET / NEW FRIENDS: _____

_____

_____

_____

FOOD, DINING & RESTAURANTS: _____

_____

_____

_____

HIGHLIGHTS / MEMORABLE EVENTS: _____

_____

_____

_____

PLACES TO GO & THINGS TO DO FOR NEXT TIME: _____

_____

_____

_____

NOTES:

Date: _____

Weather:

☀ ⛅ ☔ ❄
🌡 🌡 📢 ☁

From: _____

To: _____

Route Taken: _____

_____

Beginning Mileage: _____

Ending Mileage: _____

Total Miles Traveled: _____

CAMPGROUND INFORMATION

Name: _____

Address: _____

Phone: _____

Site #_____ $_____ ☐ Day ☐ Week ☐ Month

☐ First Visit ☐ Return Visit ☐ Easy Access
☐ Site Level ☐ Back-in ☐ Pull-through
☐ 15 amp ☐ 30 amp ☐ 50 amp
☐ Water ☐ Sewer ☐ Shade ☐ Sun
☐ Paved ☐ Sand / Grass ☐ Gravel
☐ Picnic Table ☐ Fire ring ☐ Trees ☐ Lawn
☐ Patio ☐ Kid Friendly ☐ Pet Friendly
☐ Store ☐ Cafe ☐ Firewood
☐ Ice ☐ Security ☐ Quiet ☐ Noisy

Our Rating: ☆ ☆ ☆ ☆ ☆

GPS: _____

Altitude: _____

Cell Service / Carrier: _____

☐ Antenna Reception ☐ Satellite TV ☐ Cable TV
☐ Wifi Available ☐ Free ☐ Fee $_____

Memberships: _____

Ammenities: _____

Location	☺	☺	☹	Water Pressure	☺	☺	☹
Restrooms	☺	☺	☹	Laundry	☺	☺	☹
Pool	☺	☺	☹	Hot Tub	☺	☺	☹

PLACES VISITED / ACTIVITIES: _____

_____

_____

_____

PEOPLE MET / NEW FRIENDS: _____

_____

_____

_____

FOOD, DINING & RESTAURANTS: _____

_____

_____

_____

HIGHLIGHTS / MEMORABLE EVENTS: _____

_____

_____

_____

PLACES TO GO & THINGS TO DO FOR NEXT TIME: _____

_____

_____

_____

NOTES:

Date: _____	From: _____	Beginning Mileage:

Date: _____

Weather:
☀ ⛅ ☔ ❄
🌡 🌡 📢 ☁

From: _____
To: _____
Route Taken: _____
_____

Beginning Mileage: _____

Ending Mileage: _____

Total Miles Traveled: _____

CAMPGROUND INFORMATION

Name:_____

Address:_____

Phone:_____

Site #_____ $_____ ☐ Day ☐ Week ☐ Month

☐ First Visit   ☐ Return Visit   ☐ Easy Access
☐ Site Level   ☐ Back-in   ☐ Pull-through
☐ 15 amp   ☐ 30 amp   ☐ 50 amp
☐ Water   ☐ Sewer   ☐ Shade   ☐ Sun
☐ Paved   ☐ Sand / Grass   ☐ Gravel
☐ Picnic Table ☐ Fire ring   ☐ Trees   ☐ Lawn
☐ Patio   ☐ Kid Friendly   ☐ Pet Friendly
☐ Store   ☐ Cafe   ☐ Firewood
☐ Ice   ☐ Security   ☐ Quiet   ☐ Noisy

Our Rating: ☆ ☆ ☆ ☆ ☆

GPS: _____

Altitude: _____

Cell Service / Carrier:_____

☐ Antenna Reception   ☐ Satellite TV   ☐ Cable TV
☐ Wifi Available   ☐ Free ☐ Fee $_____

Memberships: _____

Ammenities:_____

Location	☺ ☺ ☹	Water Pressure	☺ ☺ ☹
Restrooms	☺ ☺ ☹	Laundry	☺ ☺ ☹
Pool	☺ ☺ ☹	Hot Tub	☺ ☺ ☹

PLACES VISITED / ACTIVITIES: _____

_____
_____
_____

PEOPLE MET / NEW FRIENDS: _____

_____
_____
_____

FOOD, DINING & RESTAURANTS: _____

_____
_____
_____

HIGHLIGHTS / MEMORABLE EVENTS: _____

_____
_____
_____

PLACES TO GO & THINGS TO DO FOR NEXT TIME: _____

_____
_____
_____

NOTES:

Date: _____

Weather:

☀ ☁ ☔ ❄

🌡 ❄🌡 📢 ☁

From: _____

To: _____

Route Taken: _____

_____

Beginning Mileage:

_____

Ending Mileage:

_____

Total Miles Traveled:

_____

Campground Information

Name: _____

Address: _____

Phone: _____

Site #_____ $_____ ☐ Day ☐ Week ☐ Month

☐ First Visit
☐ Site Level
☐ 15 amp
☐ Water
☐ Paved
☐ Picnic Table
☐ Patio
☐ Store
☐ Ice

☐ Return Visit
☐ Back-in
☐ 30 amp
☐ Sewer
☐ Sand / Grass
☐ Fire ring
☐ Kid Friendly
☐ Cafe
☐ Security

☐ Easy Access
☐ Pull-through
☐ 50 amp
☐ Shade ☐ Sun
☐ Gravel
☐ Trees ☐ Lawn
☐ Pet Friendly
☐ Firewood
☐ Quiet ☐ Noisy

Our Rating: ☆ ☆ ☆ ☆ ☆

GPS: _____

Altitude: _____

Cell Service / Carrier: _____

☐ Antenna Reception   ☐ Satellite TV   ☐ Cable TV
☐ Wifi Available   ☐ Free ☐ Fee $_____

Memberships: _____

Ammenities: _____

Location	☺	☺	☹	Water Pressure	☺	☺	☹
Restrooms	☺	☺	☹	Laundry	☺	☺	☹
Pool	☺	☺	☹	Hot Tub	☺	☺	☹

Places Visited / Activities: _____

_____

_____

_____

People Met / New Friends: _____

_____

_____

_____

Food, Dining & Restaurants: _____

_____

_____

_____

Highlights / Memorable Events: _____

_____

_____

_____

Places To Go & Things To Do for Next Time: _____

_____

_____

_____

NOTES:

Date: _____

Weather:

☀ ☁ ☔ ❄

🌡 ❄ 📢 ☁

From: _____

To: _____

Route Taken: _____

_____

Beginning Mileage: _____

Ending Mileage: _____

Total Miles Traveled: _____

CAMPGROUND INFORMATION

Name: _____

Address: _____

Phone: _____

Site # _____ $ _____ ☐ Day ☐ Week ☐ Month

☐ First Visit   ☐ Return Visit   ☐ Easy Access
☐ Site Level   ☐ Back-in   ☐ Pull-through
☐ 15 amp   ☐ 30 amp   ☐ 50 amp
☐ Water   ☐ Sewer   ☐ Shade   ☐ Sun
☐ Paved   ☐ Sand / Grass   ☐ Gravel
☐ Picnic Table   ☐ Fire ring   ☐ Trees   ☐ Lawn
☐ Patio   ☐ Kid Friendly   ☐ Pet Friendly
☐ Store   ☐ Cafe   ☐ Firewood
☐ Ice   ☐ Security   ☐ Quiet   ☐ Noisy

Our Rating: ☆ ☆ ☆ ☆ ☆

GPS: _____

Altitude: _____

Cell Service / Carrier: _____

☐ Antenna Reception   ☐ Satellite TV   ☐ Cable TV
☐ Wifi Available   ☐ Free ☐ Fee $_____

Memberships: _____

Ammenities: _____

Location	☺	😐	☹	Water Pressure	☺	😐	☹
Restrooms	☺	😐	☹	Laundry	☺	😐	☹
Pool	☺	😐	☹	Hot Tub	☺	😐	☹

PLACES VISITED / ACTIVITIES: _____

_____

_____

_____

PEOPLE MET / NEW FRIENDS: _____

_____

_____

_____

FOOD, DINING & RESTAURANTS: _____

_____

_____

_____

HIGHLIGHTS / MEMORABLE EVENTS: _____

_____

_____

_____

PLACES TO GO & THINGS TO DO FOR NEXT TIME: _____

_____

_____

_____

NOTES:

Date: _____	From: _____	Beginning Mileage:
Weather:	To: _____	Ending Mileage:
	Route Taken: _____	
	_____	Total Miles Traveled:

CAMPGROUND INFORMATION

Name:_____

Address:_____

Phone:_____

Site #_____ $_____ ☐ Day ☐ Week ☐ Month

☐ First Visit ☐ Return Visit ☐ Easy Access
☐ Site Level ☐ Back-in ☐ Pull-through
☐ 15 amp ☐ 30 amp ☐ 50 amp
☐ Water ☐ Sewer ☐ Shade ☐ Sun
☐ Paved ☐ Sand / Grass ☐ Gravel
☐ Picnic Table ☐ Fire ring ☐ Trees ☐ Lawn
☐ Patio ☐ Kid Friendly ☐ Pet Friendly
☐ Store ☐ Cafe ☐ Firewood
☐ Ice ☐ Security ☐ Quiet ☐ Noisy

Our Rating: ☆ ☆ ☆ ☆ ☆

GPS: _____

Altitude: _____

Cell Service / Carrier:_____

☐ Antenna Reception ☐ Satellite TV ☐ Cable TV
☐ Wifi Available ☐ Free ☐ Fee $_____

Memberships: _____

Ammenities:_____

Location	☺ ☺ ☹	Water Pressure	☺ ☺ ☹
Restrooms	☺ ☺ ☹	Laundry	☺ ☺ ☹
Pool	☺ ☺ ☹	Hot Tub	☺ ☺ ☹

PLACES VISITED / ACTIVITIES: _____

_____

_____

_____

PEOPLE MET / NEW FRIENDS: _____

_____

_____

_____

FOOD, DINING & RESTAURANTS: _____

_____

_____

_____

HIGHLIGHTS / MEMORABLE EVENTS: _____

_____

_____

_____

PLACES TO GO & THINGS TO DO FOR NEXT TIME: _____

_____

_____

_____

NOTES:

Date: _____

Weather:

From: _____
To: _____
Route Taken: _____
_____

Beginning Mileage:
_____
Ending Mileage:
_____
Total Miles Traveled:

CAMPGROUND INFORMATION

Name:_____

Address:_____

Phone:_____

Site #_____ $_____ ☐ Day ☐ Week ☐ Month

☐ First Visit   ☐ Return Visit   ☐ Easy Access
☐ Site Level   ☐ Back-in   ☐ Pull-through
☐ 15 amp   ☐ 30 amp   ☐ 50 amp
☐ Water   ☐ Sewer   ☐ Shade   ☐ Sun
☐ Paved   ☐ Sand / Grass   ☐ Gravel
☐ Picnic Table   ☐ Fire ring   ☐ Trees   ☐ Lawn
☐ Patio   ☐ Kid Friendly   ☐ Pet Friendly
☐ Store   ☐ Cafe   ☐ Firewood
☐ Ice   ☐ Security   ☐ Quiet   ☐ Noisy

Our Rating: ☆ ☆ ☆ ☆ ☆

GPS: _____

Altitude: _____

Cell Service / Carrier:_____

☐ Antenna Reception   ☐ Satellite TV   ☐ Cable TV
☐ Wifi Available   ☐ Free ☐ Fee $_____

Memberships: _____

Ammenities:_____

Location	☺	☺	☹	Water Pressure	☺	☺	☹
Restrooms	☺	☺	☹	Laundry	☺	☺	☹
Pool	☺	☺	☹	Hot Tub	☺	☺	☹

PLACES VISITED / ACTIVITIES: _____
_____
_____
_____

PEOPLE MET / NEW FRIENDS: _____
_____
_____
_____

FOOD, DINING & RESTAURANTS: _____
_____
_____
_____

HIGHLIGHTS / MEMORABLE EVENTS: _____
_____
_____
_____

PLACES TO GO & THINGS TO DO FOR NEXT TIME: _____
_____
_____
_____

NOTES:

Date: _____ From: _____ Beginning Mileage: _____

Weather: To: _____

☀ ⛅ ☔ ❄ Route Taken: _____ Ending Mileage: _____

🌡 ❄ 🚩 ☁ _____ Total Miles Traveled: _____

Campground Information

Name: _____ Our Rating: ☆ ☆ ☆ ☆ ☆

Address: _____ GPS: _____

Phone: _____ Altitude: _____

Site # _____ $ _____ ☐ Day ☐ Week ☐ Month Cell Service / Carrier: _____

☐ First Visit ☐ Return Visit ☐ Easy Access ☐ Antenna Reception ☐ Satellite TV ☐ Cable TV
☐ Site Level ☐ Back-in ☐ Pull-through ☐ Wifi Available ☐ Free ☐ Fee $ _____
☐ 15 amp ☐ 30 amp ☐ 50 amp
☐ Water ☐ Sewer ☐ Shade ☐ Sun Memberships: _____
☐ Paved ☐ Sand / Grass ☐ Gravel Ammenities: _____
☐ Picnic Table ☐ Fire ring ☐ Trees ☐ Lawn Location ☺ ☺ ☹ Water Pressure ☺ ☺ ☹
☐ Patio ☐ Kid Friendly ☐ Pet Friendly Restrooms ☺ ☺ ☹ Laundry ☺ ☺ ☹
☐ Store ☐ Cafe ☐ Firewood Pool ☺ ☺ ☹ Hot Tub ☺ ☺ ☹
☐ Ice ☐ Security ☐ Quiet ☐ Noisy

Places Visited / Activities: _____

_____
_____
_____

People Met / New Friends: _____

_____
_____
_____

Food, Dining & Restaurants: _____

_____
_____
_____

Highlights / Memorable Events: _____

_____
_____
_____

Places To Go & Things To Do for Next Time: _____

_____
_____
_____

NOTES:

Date: _____	From: _____	Beginning Mileage: _____
Weather:	To: _____	Ending Mileage: _____
☀ ☁ ☂ ❄ 🌡 🌡 🚩 ☁	Route Taken: _____	Total Miles Traveled:

CAMPGROUND INFORMATION

Name:_____

Address:_____

Phone:_____

Site #_____ $_____ ☐ Day ☐ Week ☐ Month

☐ First Visit ☐ Return Visit ☐ Easy Access
☐ Site Level ☐ Back-in ☐ Pull-through
☐ 15 amp ☐ 30 amp ☐ 50 amp
☐ Water ☐ Sewer ☐ Shade ☐ Sun
☐ Paved ☐ Sand / Grass ☐ Gravel
☐ Picnic Table ☐ Fire ring ☐ Trees ☐ Lawn
☐ Patio ☐ Kid Friendly ☐ Pet Friendly
☐ Store ☐ Cafe ☐ Firewood
☐ Ice ☐ Security ☐ Quiet ☐ Noisy

Our Rating: ☆ ☆ ☆ ☆ ☆

GPS: _____

Altitude: _____

Cell Service / Carrier:_____

☐ Antenna Reception ☐ Satellite TV ☐ Cable TV
☐ Wifi Available ☐ Free ☐ Fee $_____

Memberships: _____

Ammenities:_____

Location	☺	😐	☹	Water Pressure	☺	😐	☹
Restrooms	☺	😐	☹	Laundry	☺	😐	☹
Pool	☺	😐	☹	Hot Tub	☺	😐	☹

PLACES VISITED / ACTIVITIES: _____

_____

_____

_____

PEOPLE MET / NEW FRIENDS: _____

_____

_____

_____

FOOD, DINING & RESTAURANTS: _____

_____

_____

_____

HIGHLIGHTS / MEMORABLE EVENTS: _____

_____

_____

_____

PLACES TO GO & THINGS TO DO FOR NEXT TIME: _____

_____

_____

_____

NOTES:

Date: _____

Weather:

☀ ⛅ ☔ ❄
🌡 ❄ 🎏 ☁

From: _____

To: _____

Route Taken: _____

_____

Beginning Mileage:

_____

Ending Mileage:

_____

Total Miles Traveled:

CAMPGROUND INFORMATION

Name: _____

Address: _____

Phone: _____

Site # _____ $ _____ ☐ Day ☐ Week ☐ Month

☐ First Visit
☐ Site Level
☐ 15 amp
☐ Water
☐ Paved
☐ Picnic Table
☐ Patio
☐ Store
☐ Ice

☐ Return Visit
☐ Back-in
☐ 30 amp
☐ Sewer
☐ Sand / Grass
☐ Fire ring
☐ Kid Friendly
☐ Cafe
☐ Security

☐ Easy Access
☐ Pull-through
☐ 50 amp
☐ Shade ☐ Sun
☐ Gravel
☐ Trees ☐ Lawn
☐ Pet Friendly
☐ Firewood
☐ Quiet ☐ Noisy

Our Rating: ☆ ☆ ☆ ☆ ☆

GPS: _____

Altitude: _____

Cell Service / Carrier: _____

☐ Antenna Reception   ☐ Satellite TV   ☐ Cable TV
☐ Wifi Available   ☐ Free ☐ Fee $ _____

Memberships: _____

Ammenities: _____

Location	☺	☺	☹	Water Pressure	☺	☺	☹
Restrooms	☺	☺	☹	Laundry	☺	☺	☹
Pool	☺	☺	☹	Hot Tub	☺	☺	☹

PLACES VISITED / ACTIVITIES: _____

_____

_____

_____

PEOPLE MET / NEW FRIENDS: _____

_____

_____

_____

FOOD, DINING & RESTAURANTS: _____

_____

_____

_____

HIGHLIGHTS / MEMORABLE EVENTS: _____

_____

_____

_____

PLACES TO GO & THINGS TO DO FOR NEXT TIME: _____

_____

_____

_____

NOTES:

Date: _____   From: _____   Beginning Mileage: _____

To: _____

Weather: Route Taken: _____   Ending Mileage: _____

☀ ⛅ ☔ ❄   _____   Total Miles Traveled: _____

🌡 🌡 📢 ☁

Campground Information

Name: _____   Our Rating: ☆ ☆ ☆ ☆ ☆

Address: _____   GPS: _____

Phone: _____   Altitude: _____

Site # _____ $ _____ ☐ Day ☐ Week ☐ Month   Cell Service / Carrier: _____

☐ First Visit	☐ Return Visit	☐ Easy Access	☐ Antenna Reception ☐ Satellite TV ☐ Cable TV
☐ Site Level	☐ Back-in	☐ Pull-through	☐ Wifi Available ☐ Free ☐ Fee $_____
☐ 15 amp	☐ 30 amp	☐ 50 amp	Memberships: _____
☐ Water	☐ Sewer	☐ Shade ☐ Sun	
☐ Paved	☐ Sand / Grass	☐ Gravel	Ammenities: _____
☐ Picnic Table	☐ Fire ring	☐ Trees ☐ Lawn	Location ☺ ☹ 😖 Water Pressure ☺ ☹ 😖
☐ Patio	☐ Kid Friendly	☐ Pet Friendly	Restrooms ☺ ☹ 😖 Laundry ☺ ☹ 😖
☐ Store	☐ Cafe	☐ Firewood	Pool ☺ ☹ 😖 Hot Tub ☺ ☹ 😖
☐ Ice	☐ Security	☐ Quiet ☐ Noisy	

Places Visited / Activities: _____

_____

_____

_____

People Met / New Friends: _____

_____

_____

_____

Food, Dining & Restaurants: _____

_____

_____

_____

Highlights / Memorable Events: _____

_____

_____

_____

Places To Go & Things To Do for Next Time: _____

_____

_____

_____

NOTES:

Date: _____	From: _____	Beginning Mileage:
	To: _____	Ending Mileage:
Weather:	Route Taken: _____	
☀ ⛅ ☔ ❄	_____	Total Miles Traveled:
🌡 ❄ 📯 ☁		

Campground Information

Name:_____	Our Rating: ☆ ☆ ☆ ☆ ☆
Address:_____	GPS: _____
Phone:_____	Altitude: _____
Site #_____ $_____ ☐ Day ☐ Week ☐ Month	Cell Service / Carrier:_____

Site checklist			Campground amenities
☐ First Visit	☐ Return Visit	☐ Easy Access	☐ Antenna Reception ☐ Satellite TV ☐ Cable TV
☐ Site Level	☐ Back-in	☐ Pull-through	☐ Wifi Available ☐ Free ☐ Fee $_____
☐ 15 amp	☐ 30 amp	☐ 50 amp	Memberships: _____
☐ Water	☐ Sewer	☐ Shade ☐ Sun	Ammenities:_____
☐ Paved	☐ Sand / Grass	☐ Gravel	Location ☺ 😐 ☹ Water Pressure ☺ 😐 ☹
☐ Picnic Table	☐ Fire ring	☐ Trees ☐ Lawn	Restrooms ☺ 😐 ☹ Laundry ☺ 😐 ☹
☐ Patio	☐ Kid Friendly	☐ Pet Friendly	Pool ☺ 😐 ☹ Hot Tub ☺ 😐 ☹
☐ Store	☐ Cafe	☐ Firewood	
☐ Ice	☐ Security	☐ Quiet ☐ Noisy	

Places Visited / Activities: _____

_____

_____

_____

People Met / New Friends: _____

_____

_____

_____

Food, Dining & Restaurants: _____

_____

_____

_____

Highlights / Memorable Events: _____

_____

_____

_____

Places To Go & Things To Do for Next Time: _____

_____

_____

_____

NOTES:

Date: _____

Weather:

From: _____

To: _____

Route Taken: _____

_____

Beginning Mileage:

_____

Ending Mileage:

_____

Total Miles Traveled:

_____

CAMPGROUND INFORMATION

Name: _____

Address: _____

Phone: _____

Site # _____ $ _____ ☐ Day ☐ Week ☐ Month

☐ First Visit   ☐ Return Visit   ☐ Easy Access
☐ Site Level   ☐ Back-in   ☐ Pull-through
☐ 15 amp   ☐ 30 amp   ☐ 50 amp
☐ Water   ☐ Sewer   ☐ Shade   ☐ Sun
☐ Paved   ☐ Sand / Grass   ☐ Gravel
☐ Picnic Table   ☐ Fire ring   ☐ Trees   ☐ Lawn
☐ Patio   ☐ Kid Friendly   ☐ Pet Friendly
☐ Store   ☐ Cafe   ☐ Firewood
☐ Ice   ☐ Security   ☐ Quiet   ☐ Noisy

Our Rating: ☆ ☆ ☆ ☆ ☆

GPS: _____

Altitude: _____

Cell Service / Carrier: _____

☐ Antenna Reception   ☐ Satellite TV   ☐ Cable TV
☐ Wifi Available   ☐ Free ☐ Fee $ _____

Memberships: _____

Ammenities: _____

	☺	☺	☹		☺	☺	☹
Location	☺	☺	☹	Water Pressure	☺	☺	☹
Restrooms	☺	☺	☹	Laundry	☺	☺	☹
Pool	☺	☺	☹	Hot Tub	☺	☺	☹

PLACES VISITED / ACTIVITIES: _____

_____
_____
_____

PEOPLE MET / NEW FRIENDS: _____

_____
_____
_____

FOOD, DINING & RESTAURANTS: _____

_____
_____
_____

HIGHLIGHTS / MEMORABLE EVENTS: _____

_____
_____
_____

PLACES TO GO & THINGS TO DO FOR NEXT TIME: _____

_____
_____
_____

NOTES:

Date: _____	From: _____	Beginning Mileage:
	To: _____	_____
Weather:	Route Taken: _____	Ending Mileage:
	_____	_____
		Total Miles Traveled:

Campground Information

Name: _____	Our Rating: ☆ ☆ ☆ ☆ ☆	
Address: _____	GPS: _____	
Phone: _____	Altitude: _____	

Site # _____ $ _____ ☐ Day ☐ Week ☐ Month

Cell Service / Carrier: _____

☐ First Visit	☐ Return Visit	☐ Easy Access
☐ Site Level	☐ Back-in	☐ Pull-through
☐ 15 amp	☐ 30 amp	☐ 50 amp
☐ Water	☐ Sewer	☐ Shade ☐ Sun
☐ Paved	☐ Sand / Grass	☐ Gravel
☐ Picnic Table	☐ Fire ring	☐ Trees ☐ Lawn
☐ Patio	☐ Kid Friendly	☐ Pet Friendly
☐ Store	☐ Cafe	☐ Firewood
☐ Ice	☐ Security	☐ Quiet ☐ Noisy

☐ Antenna Reception ☐ Satellite TV ☐ Cable TV
☐ Wifi Available ☐ Free ☐ Fee $_____

Memberships: _____

Ammenities: _____

Location	☺ ☺ ☹	Water Pressure	☺ ☺ ☹
Restrooms	☺ ☺ ☹	Laundry	☺ ☺ ☹
Pool	☺ ☺ ☹	Hot Tub	☺ ☺ ☹

Places Visited / Activities: _____

_____

_____

_____

People Met / New Friends: _____

_____

_____

_____

Food, Dining & Restaurants: _____

_____

_____

Highlights / Memorable Events: _____

_____

_____

Places To Go & Things To Do for Next Time: _____

_____

_____

_____

NOTES:

Date: _____	From: _____	Beginning Mileage:
	To: _____	
Weather:	Route Taken: _____	Ending Mileage:
☀ ⛅ ☔ ❄	_____	
🌡 🌡 🚩 ☁	_____	Total Miles Traveled:

CAMPGROUND INFORMATION

Name:_____	Our Rating: ☆ ☆ ☆ ☆ ☆
Address:_____	GPS: _____
Phone:_____	Altitude: _____
Site #_____ $_____ ☐ Day ☐ Week ☐ Month	Cell Service / Carrier:_____

☐ First Visit   ☐ Return Visit   ☐ Easy Access
☐ Site Level   ☐ Back-in   ☐ Pull-through
☐ 15 amp   ☐ 30 amp   ☐ 50 amp
☐ Water   ☐ Sewer   ☐ Shade   ☐ Sun
☐ Paved   ☐ Sand / Grass   ☐ Gravel
☐ Picnic Table   ☐ Fire ring   ☐ Trees   ☐ Lawn
☐ Patio   ☐ Kid Friendly   ☐ Pet Friendly
☐ Store   ☐ Cafe   ☐ Firewood
☐ Ice   ☐ Security   ☐ Quiet   ☐ Noisy

☐ Antenna Reception   ☐ Satellite TV   ☐ Cable TV
☐ Wifi Available   ☐ Free ☐ Fee $_____

Memberships: _____

Ammenities:_____

Location	☺	😐	☹	Water Pressure	☺	😐	☹
Restrooms	☺	😐	☹	Laundry	☺	😐	☹
Pool	☺	😐	☹	Hot Tub	☺	😐	☹

PLACES VISITED / ACTIVITIES: _____
_____
_____
_____

PEOPLE MET / NEW FRIENDS: _____
_____
_____
_____

FOOD, DINING & RESTAURANTS: _____
_____
_____
_____

HIGHLIGHTS / MEMORABLE EVENTS: _____
_____
_____
_____

PLACES TO GO & THINGS TO DO FOR NEXT TIME: _____
_____
_____
_____

NOTES:

Date: _____

Weather:

☀ ⛅ ☔ ❄
🌡 🌡 📢 🌀

From: _____

To: _____

Route Taken: _____

_____

Beginning Mileage:

_____

Ending Mileage:

_____

Total Miles Traveled:

CAMPGROUND INFORMATION

Name: _____

Address: _____

Phone: _____

Site # _____ $ _____ ☐ Day ☐ Week ☐ Month

☐ First Visit ☐ Return Visit ☐ Easy Access
☐ Site Level ☐ Back-in ☐ Pull-through
☐ 15 amp ☐ 30 amp ☐ 50 amp
☐ Water ☐ Sewer ☐ Shade ☐ Sun
☐ Paved ☐ Sand / Grass ☐ Gravel
☐ Picnic Table ☐ Fire ring ☐ Trees ☐ Lawn
☐ Patio ☐ Kid Friendly ☐ Pet Friendly
☐ Store ☐ Cafe ☐ Firewood
☐ Ice ☐ Security ☐ Quiet ☐ Noisy

Our Rating: ☆ ☆ ☆ ☆ ☆

GPS: _____

Altitude: _____

Cell Service / Carrier: _____

☐ Antenna Reception ☐ Satellite TV ☐ Cable TV
☐ Wifi Available ☐ Free ☐ Fee $ _____

Memberships: _____

Ammenities: _____

Location	☺	☺	☹	Water Pressure	☺	☺	☹
Restrooms	☺	☺	☹	Laundry	☺	☺	☹
Pool	☺	☺	☹	Hot Tub	☺	☺	☹

PLACES VISITED / ACTIVITIES: _____

_____

_____

_____

PEOPLE MET / NEW FRIENDS: _____

_____

_____

_____

FOOD, DINING & RESTAURANTS: _____

_____

_____

_____

HIGHLIGHTS / MEMORABLE EVENTS: _____

_____

_____

_____

PLACES TO GO & THINGS TO DO FOR NEXT TIME: _____

_____

_____

_____

NOTES:

Date: _____

Weather:
☀ ☁ 🌧 ❄
🌡 🌡 📢 ☁

From: _____

To: _____

Route Taken: _____

_____

Beginning Mileage:
_____

Ending Mileage:
_____

Total Miles Traveled:

Campground Information

Name:_____

Address:_____

Phone:_____

Site #_____ $_____ ☐ Day ☐ Week ☐ Month

☐ First Visit   ☐ Return Visit   ☐ Easy Access
☐ Site Level   ☐ Back-in   ☐ Pull-through
☐ 15 amp   ☐ 30 amp   ☐ 50 amp
☐ Water   ☐ Sewer   ☐ Shade   ☐ Sun
☐ Paved   ☐ Sand / Grass   ☐ Gravel
☐ Picnic Table ☐ Fire ring   ☐ Trees   ☐ Lawn
☐ Patio   ☐ Kid Friendly   ☐ Pet Friendly
☐ Store   ☐ Cafe   ☐ Firewood
☐ Ice   ☐ Security   ☐ Quiet   ☐ Noisy

Our Rating: ☆ ☆ ☆ ☆ ☆

GPS: _____

Altitude: _____

Cell Service / Carrier:_____

☐ Antenna Reception   ☐ Satellite TV   ☐ Cable TV
☐ Wifi Available   ☐ Free ☐ Fee $_____

Memberships: _____

Ammenities:_____

Location	☺ ☺ ☹	Water Pressure	☺ ☺ ☹
Restrooms	☺ ☺ ☹	Laundry	☺ ☺ ☹
Pool	☺ ☺ ☹	Hot Tub	☺ ☺ ☹

Places Visited / Activities: _____

_____

_____

_____

People Met / New Friends: _____

_____

_____

_____

Food, Dining & Restaurants: _____

_____

_____

_____

Highlights / Memorable Events: _____

_____

_____

_____

Places To Go & Things To Do for Next Time: _____

_____

_____

_____

NOTES:

Date: _____

Weather:

From: _____

To: _____

Route Taken: _____

_____

Beginning Mileage: _____

Ending Mileage: _____

Total Miles Traveled: _____

Campground Information

Name: _____

Address: _____

Phone: _____

Site #_____ $_____ ☐ Day ☐ Week ☐ Month

☐ First Visit   ☐ Return Visit   ☐ Easy Access
☐ Site Level   ☐ Back-in   ☐ Pull-through
☐ 15 amp   ☐ 30 amp   ☐ 50 amp
☐ Water   ☐ Sewer   ☐ Shade ☐ Sun
☐ Paved   ☐ Sand / Grass   ☐ Gravel
☐ Picnic Table   ☐ Fire ring   ☐ Trees ☐ Lawn
☐ Patio   ☐ Kid Friendly   ☐ Pet Friendly
☐ Store   ☐ Cafe   ☐ Firewood
☐ Ice   ☐ Security   ☐ Quiet ☐ Noisy

Our Rating: ☆ ☆ ☆ ☆ ☆

GPS: _____

Altitude: _____

Cell Service / Carrier: _____

☐ Antenna Reception   ☐ Satellite TV   ☐ Cable TV
☐ Wifi Available   ☐ Free ☐ Fee $_____

Memberships: _____

Ammenities: _____

Location	☺	☺	☹	Water Pressure	☺	☺	☹
Restrooms	☺	☺	☹	Laundry	☺	☺	☹
Pool	☺	☺	☹	Hot Tub	☺	☺	☹

Places Visited / Activities:

_____
_____
_____
_____

People Met / New Friends:

_____
_____
_____
_____

Food, Dining & Restaurants:

_____
_____
_____
_____

Highlights / Memorable Events:

_____
_____
_____

Places To Go & Things To Do for Next Time:

_____
_____
_____

NOTES:

Date: _____

Weather:

☀ ☁ ☂ ❄

🌡 🌡 🚩 ☁

From: _____

To: _____

Route Taken: _____

_____

Beginning Mileage:

_____

Ending Mileage:

_____

Total Miles Traveled:

_____

CAMPGROUND INFORMATION

Name: _____

Address: _____

Phone: _____

Site # _____ $ _____ ☐ Day ☐ Week ☐ Month

☐ First Visit ☐ Return Visit ☐ Easy Access
☐ Site Level ☐ Back-in ☐ Pull-through
☐ 15 amp ☐ 30 amp ☐ 50 amp
☐ Water ☐ Sewer ☐ Shade ☐ Sun
☐ Paved ☐ Sand / Grass ☐ Gravel
☐ Picnic Table ☐ Fire ring ☐ Trees ☐ Lawn
☐ Patio ☐ Kid Friendly ☐ Pet Friendly
☐ Store ☐ Cafe ☐ Firewood
☐ Ice ☐ Security ☐ Quiet ☐ Noisy

Our Rating: ☆ ☆ ☆ ☆ ☆

GPS: _____

Altitude: _____

Cell Service / Carrier: _____

☐ Antenna Reception ☐ Satellite TV ☐ Cable TV
☐ Wifi Available ☐ Free ☐ Fee $ _____

Memberships: _____

Ammenities: _____

Location	☺	☺	☹	Water Pressure	☺	☺	☹
Restrooms	☺	☺	☹	Laundry	☺	☺	☹
Pool	☺	☺	☹	Hot Tub	☺	☺	☹

PLACES VISITED / ACTIVITIES: _____

_____

_____

_____

PEOPLE MET / NEW FRIENDS: _____

_____

_____

_____

FOOD, DINING & RESTAURANTS: _____

_____

_____

_____

HIGHLIGHTS / MEMORABLE EVENTS: _____

_____

_____

_____

PLACES TO GO & THINGS TO DO FOR NEXT TIME: _____

_____

_____

_____

NOTES:

Date: _____	From: _____	Beginning Mileage:
Weather:	To: _____	Ending Mileage:
☀ ⛅ 🌧 ❄ 🌡 🌡 🚩 ☁	Route Taken: _____ _____	Total Miles Traveled:

CAMPGROUND INFORMATION

Name:_____   Our Rating: ☆ ☆ ☆ ☆ ☆

Address:_____   GPS: _____

Phone:_____   Altitude: _____

Site #_____ $_____ ☐ Day ☐ Week ☐ Month   Cell Service / Carrier:_____

☐ First Visit ☐ Return Visit ☐ Easy Access   ☐ Antenna Reception ☐ Satellite TV ☐ Cable TV
☐ Site Level ☐ Back-in ☐ Pull-through   ☐ Wifi Available ☐ Free ☐ Fee $_____
☐ 15 amp ☐ 30 amp ☐ 50 amp
☐ Water ☐ Sewer ☐ Shade ☐ Sun   Memberships: _____
☐ Paved ☐ Sand / Grass ☐ Gravel   Ammenities:_____
☐ Picnic Table ☐ Fire ring ☐ Trees ☐ Lawn
☐ Patio ☐ Kid Friendly ☐ Pet Friendly   Location ☺ ☺ ☹ Water Pressure ☺ ☺ ☹
☐ Store ☐ Cafe ☐ Firewood   Restrooms ☺ ☺ ☹ Laundry ☺ ☺ ☹
☐ Ice ☐ Security ☐ Quiet ☐ Noisy   Pool ☺ ☺ ☹ Hot Tub ☺ ☺ ☹

PLACES VISITED / ACTIVITIES: _____
_____
_____
_____

PEOPLE MET / NEW FRIENDS: _____
_____
_____
_____

FOOD, DINING & RESTAURANTS: _____
_____
_____
_____

HIGHLIGHTS / MEMORABLE EVENTS: _____
_____
_____
_____

PLACES TO GO & THINGS TO DO FOR NEXT TIME: _____
_____
_____
_____

NOTES:

Date: _____	From: _____	Beginning Mileage: _____
Weather:	To: _____	
	Route Taken: _____	Ending Mileage: _____
	_____	Total Miles Traveled: _____

CAMPGROUND INFORMATION

Name: _____

Our Rating: ☆ ☆ ☆ ☆ ☆

Address: _____

GPS: _____

Phone: _____

Altitude: _____

Site # _____ $ _____ ☐ Day ☐ Week ☐ Month

Cell Service / Carrier: _____

☐ First Visit   ☐ Return Visit   ☐ Easy Access
☐ Site Level   ☐ Back-in   ☐ Pull-through
☐ 15 amp   ☐ 30 amp   ☐ 50 amp
☐ Water   ☐ Sewer   ☐ Shade ☐ Sun
☐ Paved   ☐ Sand / Grass   ☐ Gravel
☐ Picnic Table   ☐ Fire ring   ☐ Trees ☐ Lawn
☐ Patio   ☐ Kid Friendly   ☐ Pet Friendly
☐ Store   ☐ Cafe   ☐ Firewood
☐ Ice   ☐ Security   ☐ Quiet ☐ Noisy

☐ Antenna Reception   ☐ Satellite TV   ☐ Cable TV
☐ Wifi Available   ☐ Free ☐ Fee $ _____

Memberships: _____

Ammenities: _____

Location	☺	☺	☹	Water Pressure	☺	☺	☹
Restrooms	☺	☺	☹	Laundry	☺	☺	☹
Pool	☺	☺	☹	Hot Tub	☺	☺	☹

PLACES VISITED / ACTIVITIES: _____

_____

_____

_____

PEOPLE MET / NEW FRIENDS: _____

_____

_____

_____

FOOD, DINING & RESTAURANTS: _____

_____

_____

_____

HIGHLIGHTS / MEMORABLE EVENTS: _____

_____

_____

_____

PLACES TO GO & THINGS TO DO FOR NEXT TIME: _____

_____

_____

_____

NOTES:

Date: _____

Weather:

From: _____

To: _____

Route Taken: _____

_____

Beginning Mileage:

_____

Ending Mileage:

_____

Total Miles Traveled:

_____

CAMPGROUND INFORMATION

Name: _____

Address: _____

Phone: _____

Site # _____ $ _____ ☐ Day ☐ Week ☐ Month

☐ First Visit   ☐ Return Visit   ☐ Easy Access
☐ Site Level   ☐ Back-in   ☐ Pull-through
☐ 15 amp   ☐ 30 amp   ☐ 50 amp
☐ Water   ☐ Sewer   ☐ Shade   ☐ Sun
☐ Paved   ☐ Sand / Grass   ☐ Gravel
☐ Picnic Table   ☐ Fire ring   ☐ Trees   ☐ Lawn
☐ Patio   ☐ Kid Friendly   ☐ Pet Friendly
☐ Store   ☐ Cafe   ☐ Firewood
☐ Ice   ☐ Security   ☐ Quiet   ☐ Noisy

Our Rating: ☆ ☆ ☆ ☆ ☆

GPS: _____

Altitude: _____

Cell Service / Carrier: _____

☐ Antenna Reception   ☐ Satellite TV   ☐ Cable TV
☐ Wifi Available   ☐ Free ☐ Fee $_____

Memberships: _____

Ammenities: _____

	☺	☻	☹		☺	☻	☹
Location	☺	☻	☹	Water Pressure	☺	☻	☹
Restrooms	☺	☻	☹	Laundry	☺	☻	☹
Pool	☺	☻	☹	Hot Tub	☺	☻	☹

PLACES VISITED / ACTIVITIES: _____

_____

_____

_____

PEOPLE MET / NEW FRIENDS: _____

_____

_____

_____

FOOD, DINING & RESTAURANTS: _____

_____

_____

_____

HIGHLIGHTS / MEMORABLE EVENTS: _____

_____

_____

_____

PLACES TO GO & THINGS TO DO FOR NEXT TIME: _____

_____

_____

_____

NOTES:

Date: _____

Weather:

☀ ⛅ ☔ ❄

🌡 🌡 🏴 ☁

From: _____

To: _____

Route Taken: _____

_____

Beginning Mileage:
_____

Ending Mileage:
_____

Total Miles Traveled:
_____

CAMPGROUND INFORMATION

Name: _____

Address: _____

Phone: _____

Our Rating: ☆ ☆ ☆ ☆ ☆

GPS: _____

Altitude: _____

Site # _____ $ _____ ☐ Day ☐ Week ☐ Month

☐ First Visit	☐ Return Visit	☐ Easy Access
☐ Site Level	☐ Back-in	☐ Pull-through
☐ 15 amp	☐ 30 amp	☐ 50 amp
☐ Water	☐ Sewer	☐ Shade ☐ Sun
☐ Paved	☐ Sand / Grass	☐ Gravel
☐ Picnic Table	☐ Fire ring	☐ Trees ☐ Lawn
☐ Patio	☐ Kid Friendly	☐ Pet Friendly
☐ Store	☐ Cafe	☐ Firewood
☐ Ice	☐ Security	☐ Quiet ☐ Noisy

Cell Service / Carrier: _____

☐ Antenna Reception ☐ Satellite TV ☐ Cable TV
☐ Wifi Available ☐ Free ☐ Fee $ _____

Memberships: _____

Ammenities: _____

Location	☺	😐	☹	Water Pressure	☺	😐	☹
Restrooms	☺	😐	☹	Laundry	☺	😐	☹
Pool	☺	😐	☹	Hot Tub	☺	😐	☹

PLACES VISITED / ACTIVITIES: _____

_____

_____

_____

PEOPLE MET / NEW FRIENDS: _____

_____

_____

_____

FOOD, DINING & RESTAURANTS: _____

_____

_____

_____

HIGHLIGHTS / MEMORABLE EVENTS: _____

_____

_____

_____

PLACES TO GO & THINGS TO DO FOR NEXT TIME: _____

_____

_____

_____

NOTES:

Date: _____	From: _____	Beginning Mileage:
Weather:	To: _____	Ending Mileage:
☀ ☁ ☔ ❄ 🌡 ❄ 🚩 ☁	Route Taken: _____ _____	Total Miles Traveled:

Campground Information

	Our Rating: ☆ ☆ ☆ ☆ ☆
Name:_____	GPS: _____
Address:_____	Altitude: _____
Phone:_____	Cell Service / Carrier:_____
Site #_____ $_____ ☐ Day ☐ Week ☐ Month	

☐ First Visit	☐ Return Visit	☐ Easy Access	☐ Antenna Reception ☐ Satellite TV ☐ Cable TV
☐ Site Level	☐ Back-in	☐ Pull-through	☐ Wifi Available ☐ Free ☐ Fee $_____
☐ 15 amp	☐ 30 amp	☐ 50 amp	
☐ Water	☐ Sewer	☐ Shade ☐ Sun	Memberships: _____
☐ Paved	☐ Sand / Grass	☐ Gravel	Ammenities:_____
☐ Picnic Table	☐ Fire ring	☐ Trees ☐ Lawn	Location ☺ ☺ ☹ Water Pressure ☺ ☺ ☹
☐ Patio	☐ Kid Friendly	☐ Pet Friendly	Restrooms ☺ ☺ ☹ Laundry ☺ ☺ ☹
☐ Store	☐ Cafe	☐ Firewood	Pool ☺ ☺ ☹ Hot Tub ☺ ☺ ☹
☐ Ice	☐ Security	☐ Quiet ☐ Noisy	

PLACES VISITED / ACTIVITIES: _____

_____

_____

_____

PEOPLE MET / NEW FRIENDS: _____

_____

_____

_____

FOOD, DINING & RESTAURANTS: _____

_____

_____

_____

HIGHLIGHTS / MEMORABLE EVENTS: _____

_____

_____

_____

PLACES TO GO & THINGS TO DO FOR NEXT TIME: _____

_____

_____

_____

NOTES:

Date: _____

Weather:

☀ ☁ ☂ ❄

🌡 🌡 🚩 🌩

From: _____

To: _____

Route Taken: _____

_____

Beginning Mileage:

_____

Ending Mileage:

_____

Total Miles Traveled:

_____

Campground Information

Name: _____

Address: _____

Phone: _____

Site # _____ $ _____ ☐ Day ☐ Week ☐ Month

☐ First Visit   ☐ Return Visit   ☐ Easy Access
☐ Site Level   ☐ Back-in   ☐ Pull-through
☐ 15 amp   ☐ 30 amp   ☐ 50 amp
☐ Water   ☐ Sewer   ☐ Shade   ☐ Sun
☐ Paved   ☐ Sand / Grass   ☐ Gravel
☐ Picnic Table   ☐ Fire ring   ☐ Trees   ☐ Lawn
☐ Patio   ☐ Kid Friendly   ☐ Pet Friendly
☐ Store   ☐ Cafe   ☐ Firewood
☐ Ice   ☐ Security   ☐ Quiet   ☐ Noisy

Our Rating: ☆ ☆ ☆ ☆ ☆

GPS: _____

Altitude: _____

Cell Service / Carrier: _____

☐ Antenna Reception   ☐ Satellite TV   ☐ Cable TV
☐ Wifi Available   ☐ Free ☐ Fee $_____

Memberships: _____

Ammenities: _____

	☺ ☺ ☹		☺ ☺ ☹
Location	☺ ☺ ☹	Water Pressure	☺ ☺ ☹
Restrooms	☺ ☺ ☹	Laundry	☺ ☺ ☹
Pool	☺ ☺ ☹	Hot Tub	☺ ☺ ☹

Places Visited / Activities: _____

_____
_____
_____

People Met / New Friends: _____

_____
_____
_____

Food, Dining & Restaurants: _____

_____
_____
_____

Highlights / Memorable Events: _____

_____
_____
_____

Places To Go & Things To Do for Next Time: _____

_____
_____
_____

NOTES:

Date: _____

Weather:

☀ ⛅ ☔ ❄
🌡 ❄🌡 🚩 ☁

From: _____

To: _____

Route Taken: _____
_____

Beginning Mileage:
_____

Ending Mileage:
_____

Total Miles Traveled:
_____

Campground Information

Name: _____

Address: _____

Phone: _____

Site # _____ $ _____ ☐ Day ☐ Week ☐ Month

☐ First Visit   ☐ Return Visit   ☐ Easy Access
☐ Site Level   ☐ Back-in   ☐ Pull-through
☐ 15 amp   ☐ 30 amp   ☐ 50 amp
☐ Water   ☐ Sewer   ☐ Shade ☐ Sun
☐ Paved   ☐ Sand / Grass   ☐ Gravel
☐ Picnic Table   ☐ Fire ring   ☐ Trees ☐ Lawn
☐ Patio   ☐ Kid Friendly   ☐ Pet Friendly
☐ Store   ☐ Cafe   ☐ Firewood
☐ Ice   ☐ Security   ☐ Quiet ☐ Noisy

Our Rating: ☆ ☆ ☆ ☆ ☆

GPS: _____

Altitude: _____

Cell Service / Carrier: _____

☐ Antenna Reception   ☐ Satellite TV   ☐ Cable TV
☐ Wifi Available   ☐ Free ☐ Fee $_____

Memberships: _____

Ammenities: _____

Location	☺	☺	☹	Water Pressure	☺	☺	☹
Restrooms	☺	☺	☹	Laundry	☺	☺	☹
Pool	☺	☺	☹	Hot Tub	☺	☺	☹

PLACES VISITED / ACTIVITIES: _____
_____
_____
_____

PEOPLE MET / NEW FRIENDS: _____
_____
_____
_____

FOOD, DINING & RESTAURANTS: _____
_____
_____
_____

HIGHLIGHTS / MEMORABLE EVENTS: _____
_____
_____
_____

PLACES TO GO & THINGS TO DO FOR NEXT TIME: _____
_____
_____
_____

NOTES:

Date: _____

Weather:
☀ ⛅ ☔ ❄
🌡 ❄ 🚩 ☁

From: _____

To: _____

Route Taken: _____

_____

Beginning Mileage:
_____

Ending Mileage:
_____

Total Miles Traveled:
_____

CAMPGROUND INFORMATION

Name: _____

Address: _____

Phone: _____

Site # _____ $ _____ ☐ Day ☐ Week ☐ Month

☐ First Visit
☐ Site Level
☐ 15 amp
☐ Water
☐ Paved
☐ Picnic Table
☐ Patio
☐ Store
☐ Ice

☐ Return Visit
☐ Back-in
☐ 30 amp
☐ Sewer
☐ Sand / Grass
☐ Fire ring
☐ Kid Friendly
☐ Cafe
☐ Security

☐ Easy Access
☐ Pull-through
☐ 50 amp
☐ Shade ☐ Sun
☐ Gravel
☐ Trees ☐ Lawn
☐ Pet Friendly
☐ Firewood
☐ Quiet ☐ Noisy

Our Rating: ☆ ☆ ☆ ☆ ☆

GPS: _____

Altitude: _____

Cell Service / Carrier: _____

☐ Antenna Reception ☐ Satellite TV ☐ Cable TV
☐ Wifi Available ☐ Free ☐ Fee $_____

Memberships: _____

Ammenities: _____

Location	☺	😐	☹	Water Pressure	☺	😐	☹
Restrooms	☺	😐	☹	Laundry	☺	😐	☹
Pool	☺	😐	☹	Hot Tub	☺	😐	☹

PLACES VISITED / ACTIVITIES: _____

_____

_____

_____

PEOPLE MET / NEW FRIENDS: _____

_____

_____

_____

FOOD, DINING & RESTAURANTS: _____

_____

_____

_____

HIGHLIGHTS / MEMORABLE EVENTS: _____

_____

_____

_____

PLACES TO GO & THINGS TO DO FOR NEXT TIME: _____

_____

_____

_____

NOTES:

Date: _____

Weather:

☀ ☁ ☂ ❄
🌡 🌡 🚩 ☁

From: _____

To: _____

Route Taken: _____

_____

Beginning Mileage:

_____

Ending Mileage:

_____

Total Miles Traveled:

_____

CAMPGROUND INFORMATION

Name: _____

Address: _____

Phone: _____

Site #_____ $_____ ☐ Day ☐ Week ☐ Month

☐ First Visit   ☐ Return Visit   ☐ Easy Access
☐ Site Level   ☐ Back-in   ☐ Pull-through
☐ 15 amp   ☐ 30 amp   ☐ 50 amp
☐ Water   ☐ Sewer   ☐ Shade   ☐ Sun
☐ Paved   ☐ Sand / Grass   ☐ Gravel
☐ Picnic Table   ☐ Fire ring   ☐ Trees   ☐ Lawn
☐ Patio   ☐ Kid Friendly   ☐ Pet Friendly
☐ Store   ☐ Cafe   ☐ Firewood
☐ Ice   ☐ Security   ☐ Quiet   ☐ Noisy

Our Rating: ☆ ☆ ☆ ☆ ☆

GPS: _____

Altitude: _____

Cell Service / Carrier: _____

☐ Antenna Reception   ☐ Satellite TV   ☐ Cable TV
☐ Wifi Available   ☐ Free   ☐ Fee $_____

Memberships: _____

Ammenities: _____

	☺	☺	☹		☺	☺	☹
Location	☺	☺	☹	Water Pressure	☺	☺	☹
Restrooms	☺	☺	☹	Laundry	☺	☺	☹
Pool	☺	☺	☹	Hot Tub	☺	☺	☹

PLACES VISITED / ACTIVITIES: _____

_____

_____

_____

PEOPLE MET / NEW FRIENDS: _____

_____

_____

_____

FOOD, DINING & RESTAURANTS: _____

_____

_____

_____

HIGHLIGHTS / MEMORABLE EVENTS: _____

_____

_____

_____

PLACES TO GO & THINGS TO DO FOR NEXT TIME: _____

_____

_____

_____

NOTES:

Date: _____

Weather:

☀ ⛅ ☔ ❄

🌡 ❄🌡 🚩 ☁

From: _____

To: _____

Route Taken: _____

_____

Beginning Mileage:
_____

Ending Mileage:
_____

Total Miles Traveled:
_____

CAMPGROUND INFORMATION

Name:_____

Address:_____

Phone:_____

Our Rating: ☆ ☆ ☆ ☆ ☆

GPS: _____

Altitude: _____

Site #_____ $_____ ☐ Day ☐ Week ☐ Month

☐ First Visit   ☐ Return Visit   ☐ Easy Access
☐ Site Level   ☐ Back-in   ☐ Pull-through
☐ 15 amp   ☐ 30 amp   ☐ 50 amp
☐ Water   ☐ Sewer   ☐ Shade   ☐ Sun
☐ Paved   ☐ Sand / Grass   ☐ Gravel
☐ Picnic Table   ☐ Fire ring   ☐ Trees   ☐ Lawn
☐ Patio   ☐ Kid Friendly   ☐ Pet Friendly
☐ Store   ☐ Cafe   ☐ Firewood
☐ Ice   ☐ Security   ☐ Quiet   ☐ Noisy

Cell Service / Carrier:_____

☐ Antenna Reception   ☐ Satellite TV   ☐ Cable TV
☐ Wifi Available   ☐ Free ☐ Fee $_____

Memberships: _____

Ammenities:_____

Location	☺	☺	☹	Water Pressure	☺	☺	☹
Restrooms	☺	☺	☹	Laundry	☺	☺	☹
Pool	☺	☺	☹	Hot Tub	☺	☺	☹

PLACES VISITED / ACTIVITIES: _____

_____

_____

_____

PEOPLE MET / NEW FRIENDS: _____

_____

_____

_____

FOOD, DINING & RESTAURANTS: _____

_____

_____

_____

HIGHLIGHTS / MEMORABLE EVENTS: _____

_____

_____

_____

PLACES TO GO & THINGS TO DO FOR NEXT TIME: _____

_____

_____

_____

NOTES:

Date: _____   From: _____   Beginning Mileage: _____

Weather: To: _____   Ending Mileage: _____

☀ ⛅ ☔ ❄   Route Taken: _____   Total Miles Traveled: _____

🌡 ❄ 🚩 ☁   _____

CAMPGROUND INFORMATION

Name: _____   Our Rating: ☆ ☆ ☆ ☆ ☆

Address: _____   GPS: _____

Phone: _____   Altitude: _____

Site # _____ $ _____ ☐ Day ☐ Week ☐ Month   Cell Service / Carrier: _____

☐ First Visit   ☐ Return Visit   ☐ Easy Access   ☐ Antenna Reception   ☐ Satellite TV   ☐ Cable TV
☐ Site Level   ☐ Back-in   ☐ Pull-through   ☐ Wifi Available   ☐ Free   ☐ Fee $ _____
☐ 15 amp   ☐ 30 amp   ☐ 50 amp
☐ Water   ☐ Sewer   ☐ Shade   ☐ Sun   Memberships: _____
☐ Paved   ☐ Sand / Grass   ☐ Gravel   Ammenities: _____
☐ Picnic Table   ☐ Fire ring   ☐ Trees   ☐ Lawn
☐ Patio   ☐ Kid Friendly   ☐ Pet Friendly   Location ☺ ☹ 😖   Water Pressure ☺ ☹ 😖
☐ Store   ☐ Cafe   ☐ Firewood   Restrooms ☺ ☹ 😖   Laundry ☺ ☹ 😖
☐ Ice   ☐ Security   ☐ Quiet   ☐ Noisy   Pool ☺ ☹ 😖   Hot Tub ☺ ☹ 😖

PLACES VISITED / ACTIVITIES:
_____
_____
_____
_____

PEOPLE MET / NEW FRIENDS:
_____
_____
_____
_____

FOOD, DINING & RESTAURANTS:
_____
_____
_____
_____

HIGHLIGHTS / MEMORABLE EVENTS:
_____
_____
_____

PLACES TO GO & THINGS TO DO FOR NEXT TIME:
_____
_____
_____

NOTES:

Date: _____

Weather:

☀ ☁ ☂ ❄
🌡 🌡 🚩 ☁

From: _____

To: _____

Route Taken: _____

_____

Beginning Mileage:

_____

Ending Mileage:

_____

Total Miles Traveled:

_____

CAMPGROUND INFORMATION

Name:_____

Address:_____

Phone:_____

Site #_____ $_____ ☐ Day ☐ Week ☐ Month

☐ First Visit   ☐ Return Visit   ☐ Easy Access
☐ Site Level   ☐ Back-in   ☐ Pull-through
☐ 15 amp   ☐ 30 amp   ☐ 50 amp
☐ Water   ☐ Sewer   ☐ Shade   ☐ Sun
☐ Paved   ☐ Sand / Grass   ☐ Gravel
☐ Picnic Table   ☐ Fire ring   ☐ Trees   ☐ Lawn
☐ Patio   ☐ Kid Friendly   ☐ Pet Friendly
☐ Store   ☐ Cafe   ☐ Firewood
☐ Ice   ☐ Security   ☐ Quiet   ☐ Noisy

Our Rating: ☆ ☆ ☆ ☆ ☆

GPS: _____

Altitude: _____

Cell Service / Carrier:_____

☐ Antenna Reception   ☐ Satellite TV   ☐ Cable TV
☐ Wifi Available   ☐ Free ☐ Fee $_____

Memberships: _____

Ammenities:_____

Location	☺	😐	☹	Water Pressure	☺	😐	☹
Restrooms	☺	😐	☹	Laundry	☺	😐	☹
Pool	☺	😐	☹	Hot Tub	☺	😐	☹

PLACES VISITED / ACTIVITIES: _____

_____

_____

_____

PEOPLE MET / NEW FRIENDS: _____

_____

_____

_____

FOOD, DINING & RESTAURANTS: _____

_____

_____

_____

HIGHLIGHTS / MEMORABLE EVENTS: _____

_____

_____

_____

PLACES TO GO & THINGS TO DO FOR NEXT TIME: _____

_____

_____

_____

NOTES:

Date: _____   From: _____   Beginning Mileage: _____

Weather: To: _____   Ending Mileage: _____

☀ ⛅ ☔ ❄   Route Taken: _____

🌡 ❄🌡 🚩 ☁   _____   Total Miles Traveled: _____

Campground Information

Name: _____   Our Rating: ☆ ☆ ☆ ☆ ☆

Address: _____   GPS: _____

Phone: _____   Altitude: _____

Site # _____ $ _____ ☐ Day ☐ Week ☐ Month   Cell Service / Carrier: _____

☐ First Visit ☐ Return Visit ☐ Easy Access   ☐ Antenna Reception ☐ Satellite TV ☐ Cable TV
☐ Site Level ☐ Back-in ☐ Pull-through   ☐ Wifi Available ☐ Free ☐ Fee $ _____
☐ 15 amp ☐ 30 amp ☐ 50 amp
☐ Water ☐ Sewer ☐ Shade ☐ Sun   Memberships: _____
☐ Paved ☐ Sand / Grass ☐ Gravel   Ammenities: _____
☐ Picnic Table ☐ Fire ring ☐ Trees ☐ Lawn   Location ☺ 😐 ☹   Water Pressure ☺ 😐 ☹
☐ Patio ☐ Kid Friendly ☐ Pet Friendly   Restrooms ☺ 😐 ☹   Laundry ☺ 😐 ☹
☐ Store ☐ Cafe ☐ Firewood   Pool ☺ 😐 ☹   Hot Tub ☺ 😐 ☹
☐ Ice ☐ Security ☐ Quiet ☐ Noisy

PLACES VISITED / ACTIVITIES: _____

_____

_____

_____

PEOPLE MET / NEW FRIENDS: _____

_____

_____

_____

FOOD, DINING & RESTAURANTS: _____

_____

_____

_____

HIGHLIGHTS / MEMORABLE EVENTS: _____

_____

_____

_____

PLACES TO GO & THINGS TO DO FOR NEXT TIME: _____

_____

_____

_____

NOTES:

Date: _____   From: _____   Beginning Mileage: _____

Weather: To: _____   Ending Mileage: _____

☀ ⛅ ☔ ❄   Route Taken: _____
🌡 🌡 🚩 ☁   _____   Total Miles Traveled: _____

Campground Information

Name: _____   Our Rating: ☆ ☆ ☆ ☆ ☆

Address: _____   GPS: _____

Phone: _____   Altitude: _____

Site # _____ $ _____ ☐ Day ☐ Week ☐ Month   Cell Service / Carrier: _____

☐ First Visit   ☐ Return Visit   ☐ Easy Access   ☐ Antenna Reception   ☐ Satellite TV   ☐ Cable TV
☐ Site Level   ☐ Back-in   ☐ Pull-through   ☐ Wifi Available   ☐ Free ☐ Fee $_____
☐ 15 amp   ☐ 30 amp   ☐ 50 amp
☐ Water   ☐ Sewer   ☐ Shade ☐ Sun   Memberships: _____
☐ Paved   ☐ Sand / Grass   ☐ Gravel   Ammenities: _____
☐ Picnic Table   ☐ Fire ring   ☐ Trees ☐ Lawn   Location   ☺ ☺ ☹   Water Pressure ☺ ☺ ☹
☐ Patio   ☐ Kid Friendly   ☐ Pet Friendly   Restrooms   ☺ ☺ ☹   Laundry   ☺ ☺ ☹
☐ Store   ☐ Cafe   ☐ Firewood   Pool   ☺ ☺ ☹   Hot Tub   ☺ ☺ ☹
☐ Ice   ☐ Security   ☐ Quiet ☐ Noisy

PLACES VISITED / ACTIVITIES: _____

_____
_____
_____

PEOPLE MET / NEW FRIENDS: _____

_____
_____
_____

FOOD, DINING & RESTAURANTS: _____

_____
_____
_____

HIGHLIGHTS / MEMORABLE EVENTS: _____

_____
_____
_____

PLACES TO GO & THINGS TO DO FOR NEXT TIME: _____

_____
_____
_____

NOTES:

Date: _____

Weather:

☀ ☁ ☂ ❄
🌡 ❄ 🚩 ☁

From: _____

To: _____

Route Taken: _____

_____

Beginning Mileage:
_____

Ending Mileage:
_____

Total Miles Traveled:
_____

CAMPGROUND INFORMATION

Name: _____

Address: _____

Phone: _____

Site # _____ $ _____ ☐ Day ☐ Week ☐ Month

☐ First Visit   ☐ Return Visit   ☐ Easy Access
☐ Site Level   ☐ Back-in   ☐ Pull-through
☐ 15 amp   ☐ 30 amp   ☐ 50 amp
☐ Water   ☐ Sewer   ☐ Shade   ☐ Sun
☐ Paved   ☐ Sand / Grass   ☐ Gravel
☐ Picnic Table   ☐ Fire ring   ☐ Trees   ☐ Lawn
☐ Patio   ☐ Kid Friendly   ☐ Pet Friendly
☐ Store   ☐ Cafe   ☐ Firewood
☐ Ice   ☐ Security   ☐ Quiet   ☐ Noisy

Our Rating: ☆ ☆ ☆ ☆ ☆

GPS: _____

Altitude: _____

Cell Service / Carrier: _____

☐ Antenna Reception   ☐ Satellite TV   ☐ Cable TV
☐ Wifi Available   ☐ Free ☐ Fee $ _____

Memberships: _____

Ammenities: _____

Location   ☺ ☺ ☹   Water Pressure ☺ ☺ ☹
Restrooms   ☺ ☺ ☹   Laundry   ☺ ☺ ☹
Pool   ☺ ☺ ☹   Hot Tub   ☺ ☺ ☹

PLACES VISITED / ACTIVITIES: _____

_____

_____

_____

PEOPLE MET / NEW FRIENDS: _____

_____

_____

_____

FOOD, DINING & RESTAURANTS: _____

_____

_____

_____

HIGHLIGHTS / MEMORABLE EVENTS: _____

_____

_____

_____

PLACES TO GO & THINGS TO DO FOR NEXT TIME: _____

_____

_____

_____

NOTES:

Date: _____

Weather:

☀ ☁ ☂ ❄
🌡 ❄🌡 🚩 ☁

From: _____

To: _____

Route Taken: _____

_____

Beginning Mileage: _____

Ending Mileage: _____

Total Miles Traveled: _____

CAMPGROUND INFORMATION

Name: _____

Address: _____

Phone: _____

Site # _____ $ _____ ☐ Day ☐ Week ☐ Month

☐ First Visit ☐ Return Visit ☐ Easy Access
☐ Site Level ☐ Back-in ☐ Pull-through
☐ 15 amp ☐ 30 amp ☐ 50 amp
☐ Water ☐ Sewer ☐ Shade ☐ Sun
☐ Paved ☐ Sand / Grass ☐ Gravel
☐ Picnic Table ☐ Fire ring ☐ Trees ☐ Lawn
☐ Patio ☐ Kid Friendly ☐ Pet Friendly
☐ Store ☐ Cafe ☐ Firewood
☐ Ice ☐ Security ☐ Quiet ☐ Noisy

Our Rating: ☆ ☆ ☆ ☆ ☆

GPS: _____

Altitude: _____

Cell Service / Carrier: _____

☐ Antenna Reception ☐ Satellite TV ☐ Cable TV
☐ Wifi Available ☐ Free ☐ Fee $_____

Memberships: _____

Ammenities: _____

	☺	☻	☹		☺	☻	☹
Location	☺	☻	☹	Water Pressure	☺	☻	☹
Restrooms	☺	☻	☹	Laundry	☺	☻	☹
Pool	☺	☻	☹	Hot Tub	☺	☻	☹

PLACES VISITED / ACTIVITIES: _____

_____

_____

_____

PEOPLE MET / NEW FRIENDS: _____

_____

_____

_____

FOOD, DINING & RESTAURANTS: _____

_____

_____

_____

HIGHLIGHTS / MEMORABLE EVENTS: _____

_____

_____

_____

PLACES TO GO & THINGS TO DO FOR NEXT TIME: _____

_____

_____

_____

NOTES:

Date: _____

Weather:
☀ ⛅ ☂ ❄
🌡 🌡 🚩 ☁

From: _____

To: _____

Route Taken: _____
_____

Beginning Mileage: _____

Ending Mileage: _____

Total Miles Traveled: _____

Campground Information

Name:_____

Address:_____

Phone:_____

Site #_____ $_____ ☐ Day ☐ Week ☐ Month

☐ First Visit   ☐ Return Visit   ☐ Easy Access
☐ Site Level   ☐ Back-in   ☐ Pull-through
☐ 15 amp   ☐ 30 amp   ☐ 50 amp
☐ Water   ☐ Sewer   ☐ Shade   ☐ Sun
☐ Paved   ☐ Sand / Grass   ☐ Gravel
☐ Picnic Table   ☐ Fire ring   ☐ Trees   ☐ Lawn
☐ Patio   ☐ Kid Friendly   ☐ Pet Friendly
☐ Store   ☐ Cafe   ☐ Firewood
☐ Ice   ☐ Security   ☐ Quiet   ☐ Noisy

Our Rating: ☆ ☆ ☆ ☆ ☆

GPS: _____

Altitude: _____

Cell Service / Carrier:_____

☐ Antenna Reception   ☐ Satellite TV   ☐ Cable TV
☐ Wifi Available   ☐ Free ☐ Fee $_____

Memberships: _____

Ammenities:_____

Location	☺	😐	☹	Water Pressure	☺	😐	☹
Restrooms	☺	😐	☹	Laundry	☺	😐	☹
Pool	☺	😐	☹	Hot Tub	☺	😐	☹

Places Visited / Activities: _____
_____
_____
_____

People Met / New Friends: _____
_____
_____
_____

Food, Dining & Restaurants: _____
_____
_____
_____

Highlights / Memorable Events: _____
_____
_____
_____

Places To Go & Things To Do for Next Time: _____
_____
_____
_____

NOTES:

Date: _____	From: _____	Beginning Mileage:
Weather:	To: _____	_____
	Route Taken: _____	Ending Mileage:
	_____	_____
		Total Miles Traveled:

CAMPGROUND INFORMATION

Name: _____

Our Rating: ☆ ☆ ☆ ☆ ☆

Address: _____

GPS: _____

Phone: _____

Altitude: _____

Site # _____ $ _____ ☐ Day ☐ Week ☐ Month

Cell Service / Carrier: _____

☐ First Visit ☐ Return Visit ☐ Easy Access
☐ Site Level ☐ Back-in ☐ Pull-through
☐ 15 amp ☐ 30 amp ☐ 50 amp
☐ Water ☐ Sewer ☐ Shade ☐ Sun
☐ Paved ☐ Sand / Grass ☐ Gravel
☐ Picnic Table ☐ Fire ring ☐ Trees ☐ Lawn
☐ Patio ☐ Kid Friendly ☐ Pet Friendly
☐ Store ☐ Cafe ☐ Firewood
☐ Ice ☐ Security ☐ Quiet ☐ Noisy

☐ Antenna Reception ☐ Satellite TV ☐ Cable TV
☐ Wifi Available ☐ Free ☐ Fee $ _____

Memberships: _____

Ammenities: _____

Location	☺	☺	☹	Water Pressure	☺	☺	☹
Restrooms	☺	☺	☹	Laundry	☺	☺	☹
Pool	☺	☺	☹	Hot Tub	☺	☺	☹

PLACES VISITED / ACTIVITIES: _____

_____

_____

_____

PEOPLE MET / NEW FRIENDS: _____

_____

_____

_____

FOOD, DINING & RESTAURANTS: _____

_____

_____

_____

HIGHLIGHTS / MEMORABLE EVENTS: _____

_____

_____

_____

PLACES TO GO & THINGS TO DO FOR NEXT TIME: _____

_____

_____

_____

NOTES:

Date: _____

Weather:

☀ ⛅ ☂ ❄

🌡 ❄🌡 🚩 ☁

From: _____

To: _____

Route Taken: _____

_____

Beginning Mileage:
_____

Ending Mileage:
_____

Total Miles Traveled:
_____

CAMPGROUND INFORMATION

Name: _____

Address: _____

Phone: _____

Site # _____ $ _____ ☐ Day ☐ Week ☐ Month

☐ First Visit   ☐ Return Visit   ☐ Easy Access
☐ Site Level   ☐ Back-in   ☐ Pull-through
☐ 15 amp   ☐ 30 amp   ☐ 50 amp
☐ Water   ☐ Sewer   ☐ Shade ☐ Sun
☐ Paved   ☐ Sand / Grass   ☐ Gravel
☐ Picnic Table   ☐ Fire ring   ☐ Trees ☐ Lawn
☐ Patio   ☐ Kid Friendly   ☐ Pet Friendly
☐ Store   ☐ Cafe   ☐ Firewood
☐ Ice   ☐ Security   ☐ Quiet ☐ Noisy

Our Rating: ☆ ☆ ☆ ☆ ☆

GPS: _____

Altitude: _____

Cell Service / Carrier: _____

☐ Antenna Reception   ☐ Satellite TV   ☐ Cable TV
☐ Wifi Available   ☐ Free ☐ Fee $ _____

Memberships: _____

Ammenities: _____

Location	☺	😐	☹	Water Pressure	☺	😐	☹
Restrooms	☺	😐	☹	Laundry	☺	😐	☹
Pool	☺	😐	☹	Hot Tub	☺	😐	☹

PLACES VISITED / ACTIVITIES: _____

_____

_____

_____

PEOPLE MET / NEW FRIENDS: _____

_____

_____

_____

FOOD, DINING & RESTAURANTS: _____

_____

_____

_____

HIGHLIGHTS / MEMORABLE EVENTS: _____

_____

_____

_____

PLACES TO GO & THINGS TO DO FOR NEXT TIME: _____

_____

_____

_____

NOTES:

Date: _____	From: _____	Beginning Mileage:
Weather:	To: _____	_____
	Route Taken: _____	Ending Mileage:
	_____	_____
		Total Miles Traveled:

CAMPGROUND INFORMATION

Name:_____

Our Rating: ☆ ☆ ☆ ☆ ☆

Address:_____

GPS: _____

Phone:_____

Altitude: _____

Site #_____ $_____ ☐ Day ☐ Week ☐ Month

Cell Service / Carrier:_____

☐ First Visit ☐ Return Visit ☐ Easy Access
☐ Site Level ☐ Back-in ☐ Pull-through
☐ 15 amp ☐ 30 amp ☐ 50 amp
☐ Water ☐ Sewer ☐ Shade ☐ Sun
☐ Paved ☐ Sand / Grass ☐ Gravel
☐ Picnic Table ☐ Fire ring ☐ Trees ☐ Lawn
☐ Patio ☐ Kid Friendly ☐ Pet Friendly
☐ Store ☐ Cafe ☐ Firewood
☐ Ice ☐ Security ☐ Quiet ☐ Noisy

☐ Antenna Reception ☐ Satellite TV ☐ Cable TV
☐ Wifi Available ☐ Free ☐ Fee $_____

Memberships: _____

Ammenities:_____

Location	☺ ☺ ☹	Water Pressure	☺ ☺ ☹
Restrooms	☺ ☺ ☹	Laundry	☺ ☺ ☹
Pool	☺ ☺ ☹	Hot Tub	☺ ☺ ☹

PLACES VISITED / ACTIVITIES: _____

_____

_____

_____

PEOPLE MET / NEW FRIENDS: _____

_____

_____

_____

FOOD, DINING & RESTAURANTS: _____

_____

_____

_____

HIGHLIGHTS / MEMORABLE EVENTS: _____

_____

_____

_____

PLACES TO GO & THINGS TO DO FOR NEXT TIME: _____

_____

_____

_____

NOTES:

Date: _____	From: _____	Beginning Mileage:
Weather:	To: _____	_____
	Route Taken: _____	Ending Mileage:
	_____	_____
		Total Miles Traveled:
		_____

CAMPGROUND INFORMATION

Name:_____

Address:_____

Phone:_____

Site #_____ $_____ ☐ Day ☐ Week ☐ Month

☐ First Visit ☐ Return Visit ☐ Easy Access
☐ Site Level ☐ Back-in ☐ Pull-through
☐ 15 amp ☐ 30 amp ☐ 50 amp
☐ Water ☐ Sewer ☐ Shade ☐ Sun
☐ Paved ☐ Sand / Grass ☐ Gravel
☐ Picnic Table ☐ Fire ring ☐ Trees ☐ Lawn
☐ Patio ☐ Kid Friendly ☐ Pet Friendly
☐ Store ☐ Cafe ☐ Firewood
☐ Ice ☐ Security ☐ Quiet ☐ Noisy

Our Rating: ☆ ☆ ☆ ☆ ☆

GPS: _____

Altitude: _____

Cell Service / Carrier:_____

☐ Antenna Reception ☐ Satellite TV ☐ Cable TV
☐ Wifi Available ☐ Free ☐ Fee $_____

Memberships: _____

Ammenities:_____

Location	☺	☺	☹	Water Pressure	☺	☺	☹
Restrooms	☺	☺	☹	Laundry	☺	☺	☹
Pool	☺	☺	☹	Hot Tub	☺	☺	☹

PLACES VISITED / ACTIVITIES: _____

_____

_____

_____

PEOPLE MET / NEW FRIENDS: _____

_____

_____

_____

FOOD, DINING & RESTAURANTS: _____

_____

_____

_____

HIGHLIGHTS / MEMORABLE EVENTS: _____

_____

_____

_____

PLACES TO GO & THINGS TO DO FOR NEXT TIME: _____

_____

_____

_____

NOTES:

Date: _____	From: _____	Beginning Mileage: _____
Weather:	To: _____	Ending Mileage: _____
☀ ☁ ☂ ❄ 🌡 🌡 📣 ☁	Route Taken: _____ _____	Total Miles Traveled:

CAMPGROUND INFORMATION

Name:_____

Address:_____

Phone:_____

Site #_____ $_____ ☐ Day ☐ Week ☐ Month

☐ First Visit   ☐ Return Visit   ☐ Easy Access
☐ Site Level   ☐ Back-in   ☐ Pull-through
☐ 15 amp   ☐ 30 amp   ☐ 50 amp
☐ Water   ☐ Sewer   ☐ Shade ☐ Sun
☐ Paved   ☐ Sand / Grass   ☐ Gravel
☐ Picnic Table ☐ Fire ring   ☐ Trees ☐ Lawn
☐ Patio   ☐ Kid Friendly   ☐ Pet Friendly
☐ Store   ☐ Cafe   ☐ Firewood
☐ Ice   ☐ Security   ☐ Quiet ☐ Noisy

Our Rating: ☆ ☆ ☆ ☆ ☆

GPS: _____

Altitude: _____

Cell Service / Carrier:_____

☐ Antenna Reception   ☐ Satellite TV   ☐ Cable TV
☐ Wifi Available   ☐ Free ☐ Fee $_____

Memberships: _____

Ammenities:_____

Location	☺	☺	☹	Water Pressure	☺	☺	☹
Restrooms	☺	☺	☹	Laundry	☺	☺	☹
Pool	☺	☺	☹	Hot Tub	☺	☺	☹

PLACES VISITED / ACTIVITIES: _____

_____

_____

_____

PEOPLE MET / NEW FRIENDS: _____

_____

_____

_____

FOOD, DINING & RESTAURANTS: _____

_____

_____

_____

HIGHLIGHTS / MEMORABLE EVENTS: _____

_____

_____

_____

PLACES TO GO & THINGS TO DO FOR NEXT TIME: _____

_____

_____

_____

NOTES:

Date: _____	From: _____	Beginning Mileage:
	To: _____	
Weather:	Route Taken: _____	Ending Mileage:
☀ ⛅ ☔ ❄	_____	
🌡 🌡 🚩 ☁	_____	Total Miles Traveled:

CAMPGROUND INFORMATION

Name:_____	Our Rating: ☆ ☆ ☆ ☆ ☆
Address:_____	GPS: _____
Phone:_____	Altitude: _____
Site #_____ $_____ ☐ Day ☐ Week ☐ Month	Cell Service / Carrier:_____

☐ First Visit	☐ Return Visit	☐ Easy Access	☐ Antenna Reception ☐ Satellite TV ☐ Cable TV
☐ Site Level	☐ Back-in	☐ Pull-through	☐ Wifi Available ☐ Free ☐ Fee $_____
☐ 15 amp	☐ 30 amp	☐ 50 amp	Memberships: _____
☐ Water	☐ Sewer	☐ Shade ☐ Sun	
☐ Paved	☐ Sand / Grass	☐ Gravel	Ammenities:_____
☐ Picnic Table	☐ Fire ring	☐ Trees ☐ Lawn	Location ☺ ☺ ☹ Water Pressure ☺ ☺ ☹
☐ Patio	☐ Kid Friendly	☐ Pet Friendly	Restrooms ☺ ☺ ☹ Laundry ☺ ☺ ☹
☐ Store	☐ Cafe	☐ Firewood	Pool ☺ ☺ ☹ Hot Tub ☺ ☺ ☹
☐ Ice	☐ Security	☐ Quiet ☐ Noisy	

PLACES VISITED / ACTIVITIES: _____

_____

_____

_____

PEOPLE MET / NEW FRIENDS: _____

_____

_____

_____

FOOD, DINING & RESTAURANTS: _____

_____

_____

_____

HIGHLIGHTS / MEMORABLE EVENTS: _____

_____

_____

_____

PLACES TO GO & THINGS TO DO FOR NEXT TIME: _____

_____

_____

_____

NOTES:

Made in United States
Troutdale, OR
06/23/2023

10761057R00066